IMAGES
of America

THE PEABODY
HOTEL

PEABODY HOTEL

THE CURRENT PEABODY HOTEL. This is a postcard of the current Peabody Hotel.

IMAGES
of America

THE PEABODY HOTEL

Scott Faragher and Katherine Harrington

ARCADIA
PUBLISHING

Published by Arcadia Publishing

Charleston SC, Chicago IL, Portsmouth NH, San Francisco CA

Printed in the United States of America

Library of Congress Catalog Card Number: 2002105525

For all general information contact Arcadia Publishing at:
Telephone 843-853-2070
Fax 843-853-0044
E-mail sales@arcadiapublishing.com
For customer service and orders:
Toll-Free 1-888-313-2665

Visit us on the Internet at www.arcadiapublishing.com

Dedicated to the Belz Family

CONTENTS

ACKNOWLEDGMENTS

Special thanks to Jack Belz for proofreading the manuscript, and to Judy Wesley, who kindly and graciously granted us access to everything we needed. Thanks also to Nakita Flynn, director of public relations for the Peabody; Sharyn Burson, director of advertising for the Peabody; Greg Herning; and Linda Greenwald. Thanks also to Traci Cochran at Kinko's on Union; Patricia LaPointe of the Memphis and Shelby County Room at the new Memphis-Shelby County Public Library on Poplar; and to her husband Jack McFarland, chief architect of the Peabody's restoration. Thanks also to Henry Juszkiewicz at Gibson USA, makers of the world's finest guitars, basses, and mandolins. Be sure and visit the Lucille plant and the Smithsonian's Memphis Rock n' Soul Museum in the Beale Street Entertainment District. Thanks also to Hal and Bernard Lansky, clothiers to the King, who initially suggested this project; Gary Feder, Ewell McKee, and Mary Martin at Hunter Fan; Chad Selden; Clay Yager; Bard and W. Selden; and Kingsley Hooker.

HORSE AND CARRIAGE AT THE PEABODY. The horse and carriage seen here are reminiscent of the tradition and elegance established when the original Peabody Hotel opened in Memphis in 1869.

FOREWORD

It is normally stated that a building is simply a structure that can be architecturally attractive or unattractive, that it is basically a combination of bricks, stone, concrete, wood, paint, etc. In truth, a building is much more than that. There are certain great buildings in the world which are symbols of countries. These include for example, the White House, Buckingham Palace, and the Kremlin, among others. There are also buildings such as the Peabody Hotel, which represent a certain period in architecture and an excellence of design and quality of building materials, but much more than that, a repository of memories. The Peabody Hotel in Memphis is a treasure that has been, and is currently, enjoyed by millions of people. Events of past graduations are remembered with nostalgia—weddings, proms, dinners, rooftop dancing, and other significant events, each with its own personal memories. With its extraordinary lobby, welcoming atmosphere, and timeless character, it is a place where you relive old memories and make new ones.

When my parents, of blessed memory, Philip and Sarah Belz, were to be married, they tried unsuccessfully to have the event at the Peabody but it was booked. Almost all of the social events of great significance to my wife and me (and countless others) took place at the Peabody Hotel. This included our own wedding reception in the Continental Ballroom, which we remember almost as yesterday, even though it was some 54 years ago. Since our marriage, countless thousands of people have similarly made new memories which they relive constantly when visiting "their Peabody."

When we acquired the Peabody, it was a very sad moment in the history of our city. It was not too many years after the tragic assassination of Dr. Martin Luther King, no more than about a mile from the hotel. There was a general real estate recession then. The ravages of the rampages that followed the assassination in the form of boarded-up stores and the accelerating exodus of offices from downtown had left many businesses foreclosed and shuttered—the Peabody was among them. When we acquired it, most had concluded that it should be razed because it was an architectural dinosaur, a relic of the past, but not the future. Each time we visited and toured it, we became more and more in love with it, and resolved that it would not be torn down, but rather, would be renewed and brought back to a condition far nicer than it ever was in its heyday. We are gratified—more than that—overjoyed, that we have been blessed with the resolve and ability to accomplish that and even more. We've added to the hotel. We have continuously improved it and refined it as one does in cutting and polishing a fine diamond. In addition, early on we knew that we had to do more than simply reopen the Peabody—that we must create a new centrality in downtown, the reverberations from which would help energize the redevelopment of our downtown, and even the enlargement of it. All of this has and is occurring and was already in play as the new millennium came.

The Peabody Place project is an eight-block development extending from the Peabody to Beale Street and from the waterfront east, almost to Danny Thomas Boulevard. It is now open and drawing thousands daily with the great variety of opportunities for living, working, entertaining, exercising, and general enjoyment. Now in place are Mud Island, with its many award-winning residential communities; the rebuilt South Bluffs, with exquisite river view homes; a vibrant St. Jude Hospital and Research Center growing daily; the expanded Convention Center; the AutoZone Ballpark; and now the commencement of construction of the new NBA Arena. These are only some of the elements of the reemerging and vibrant downtown which has become again the cultural, financial, and entertainment capital of the Mid-South—and always with its crown jewel, the Peabody, at its center.

—Jack Belz

Note from Authors

It is worth mentioning that a civilization is usually fairly well represented by its architecture. Much of the American architecture of the past is in danger. Considering what has been lost already, buildings, homes, and even warehouse structures from the late 1800s and early 1900s have become increasingly significant. During the early development of American cities, if some former landmark, or even some old residence or building which had outlived its original purpose was destroyed in the name of progress, it wasn't that important. Whatever came along to replace it would no doubt be even better. Up to a point this was true. It was probably true through the 1930s. With some exceptions, the architecture of today, both residential and commercial, has degenerated in favor of cost effectiveness. Gone are the ornate stone carvings and marble columns of yesteryear, replaced by cement blocks, chrome, glass, and aluminum or vinyl siding. It is important that individuals become involved in the effort to save what's left. To that end, I urge you to join whatever organizations exist in your own cities which endeavor to preserve the physical remnants of our common heritage. They can always use volunteers, money, and the strength of numbers. In Memphis, there is Memphis Heritage, Inc., a non-profit organization dedicated to historic preservation. Their website is www.memphisheritage.org. Check it out.

INTRODUCTION

The History of the Peabody Hotel, while very interesting, is fairly cut and dry in terms of certain memorable dates, but much information about other Memphis hotels of the period is not as clear. My sources as an author for the information presented herein are from a variety of places, including personal knowledge, period press articles, reference books, and personal interviews. But some of the especially early dates and data regarding other early Memphis hotels are conflicting. An example of this is found in Joseph Isele's brief work entitled "The History of Memphis Hotels from 1823 to 1929." Isele and his brothers owned or leased several hotels in the early days of Memphis, including the original Peabody, so his information should be accurate. Regarding the former Claridge Hotel, for example, he notes that it was built in 1922 on the former site of the Arlington. He then says on the same page, two paragraphs later, that the Arlington Hotel opened on June 1, 1924. He also states that the Claridge Hotel had 557 rooms, while on the back of a period postcard of the Claridge, it says that it has 400 rooms. Dates vary from source to source as well. Did the original Gayoso open in 1842 or 1843, for example? I mention this only so that the reader will not consider my reference to Memphis hotels other than the Peabody to be definitive. This is rather an attempt to provide the interested reader with an accurate and informative history of Memphis's most famous landmark, the Peabody Hotel. The inclusion of other hotels of the same or earlier periods serves merely as a backdrop for the interest of the reader. Memphis still has several large hotels remaining from the 1920s such as the Parkview, now a retirement home; the Chisca, which is empty; the Claridge; and William Len, now apartment buildings; and, of course, the Peabody, the only one of the great Memphis hotels still serving in its original capacity. Other, older hotels such as the Marquette, Forest Park, Plaza Hotel, the King Cotton, the Arlington, and others are gone altogether and generally forgotten.

Some of the images included within the text are not of the highest quality. This is not the fault of the publisher. The authors apologize for this, but in many instances, some of these images are the only ones known to exist. Some of them are very old, and consequently not in the best condition. It was decided that the reader would probably prefer to see them, regardless of condition.

One

A TRADITION BEGINS

The Peabody Hotel in Memphis is known worldwide for its famous marble fountain and swimming ducks. And while it is the ducks which immediately come to mind when The Peabody Hotel is mentioned, the hotel is really most famous for its history and long tradition of magnificent and elegant service. Most people assume that the grand Peabody Hotel at Second and Union is the original Peabody Hotel. Considering its massive size and imposing presence, it's easy to understand why. It looks like something that has always been there. For all but a few Memphians, and indeed for most Americans, it is The Peabody Hotel. But the current Peabody, built in 1925, is actually Memphis's second Peabody Hotel, and has its roots in an earlier structure, which was built in 1869.

The name of George Peabody is especially significant in Tennessee, both in Memphis and Nashville. In Memphis, there is of course the Peabody Hotel, but there is also a major thoroughfare named in his honor, as well as Peabody Park. In Nashville there is a Peabody Street, but more significantly the George Peabody College for Teachers, now a part of the Vanderbilt University system, was named in his honor and founded with his donations. George Peabody is usually referred to simply as a "philanthropist" and that's as far as it goes. But since his name graces the subject of this book, something more should be said about him. George Peabody was born in Massachusetts in 1795 and began working as a youth at a local dry goods store. He moved to Washington, D.C., then to Baltimore. He moved to London, England in 1837 and established George Peabody and Co., where he became extremely successful in dealing with financial matters between various American and English companies. Most of his large fortune was spent in charitable and philanthropic endeavors, including funds which either created or supported a number of projects. Among them were the George Peabody College for Teachers in Nashville, the Peabody Institute of Baltimore, the Peabody Museum of Natural History at Yale, and the Peabody Museum of Archaeology and Ethnology at Harvard. Most significant was his establishment of the Peabody Fund in 1867 to further education in the war-torn South. Peabody died in London on November 4, 1869.

Many post–Civil War hotels in major cities throughout the nation opened with pomp and circumstance, and the Peabody was destined for greatness from the very beginning. In the early days of American hotels, luxuries were few. Indeed, nearly all of the modern amenities, which the American traveler of today takes for granted, were rarely available, even in the best hotels before the War Between the States. Even after the war, few hotels had private bathrooms. Bathrooms were usually found one or two per floor, at the end of the hall. Hotels were generally cold in the winter and hot in the summer, with little of the creature comforts provided by modern engineering. There were also problems with fire and natural gas, and hotels of the period frequently burned. Many travelers died simply trying to get a good night's sleep. Consequently, when the original Peabody Hotel opened with 75 individual rooms, each with its own private bathroom, it was considered luxurious. The $60,000 hotel also contained a saloon, a ballroom, and a lobby. Room prices during this initial period were $4 per day and included meals, a practice which sadly no longer exists. Gas lights and open fires in the room's fireplace cost extra as they did in most hotels of the day. In fact, a 1934 article in the Memphis Press-Scimitar related the following: "John T. Wilkinson of the National Bank of Commerce has a bill which Alfred D. Carter, Marion, Ark., found in some old papers recently. It bears the date of Feb. 2, 1869 when the Peabody was then at Main and Monroe, and was owned by D. Cockrell & Sons. It showed that Mrs. P.A. Cox owed the hotel $28 for one week's board, $14 for her child's board, $1.75 for gas, and $3. for `fire in the room' making a total of $46.75 for the week."

PEABODY HOTEL, MEMPHIS.
In the Heart of the Business, Shopping and Skyscraper District of the City.

Postcard of Original Peabody Hotel.

13

THE FIRST PEABODY HOTEL. The first Peabody Hotel was named in honor of philanthropist George Peabody by the hotel's builder Robert Campbell Brinkley, a lawyer and businessman who moved to Memphis from Nashville in 1842. As the story is told, Brinkley was on his way to England in search of a loan to aid his troubled railroad when he met the famous George Peabody aboard ship. They developed a friendship and Peabody subsequently helped Brinkley get his railroad back on track. With his finances secure, Brinkley turned his attention to the creation of a grand hotel in Memphis, which he named in his benefactor George Peabody's honor. The original Peabody Hotel opened on February 6, 1869, at Main and Monroe, amidst much fanfare with a grand celebration attended by 200 of the city's most prominent couples.

THE LOBBY OF THE FIRST PEABODY. The lobby was as magnificent as it was massive. Robert Brinkley, with the earlier help of George Peabody, succeeded in creating a grand and modern hotel for this prosperous post-war Southern city, a hotel which would serve well into the next century. The Peabody was then given as a wedding gift by Brinkley to his daughter, Annie Overton Brinkley, upon the occasion of her marriage to Robert Snowden. By 1876, the Peabody was again in the hands of its original owner, Brinkley, who hired C. Galloway, former chief of staff at the Gayoso as manager.

THE LOBBY OF THE FIRST PEABODY. The arched doorways gave the lobby a Moorish feel. The history of the Peabody Hotel is in many ways intertwined with that of the city of Memphis itself. Local newspapers of the time, such as the *Daily Post* and the *Public Ledger*, eagerly noted when famous citizens like Nathan Bedford Forrest, Robert E. Lee, Andrew Johnson, and other important citizens of the era visited Memphis and stayed at the Peabody. The hotel was frequently the site of many significant social events as well, including balls, dinners, and gatherings of the Memphis bon ton. Perhaps the most famous of all its festivities was the Memphis reunion of Confederate soldiers in 1901. On this occasion, the Peabody served as the headquarters for this historic veterans reunion, which brought in excess of 165,000 former Confederate soldiers to the city.

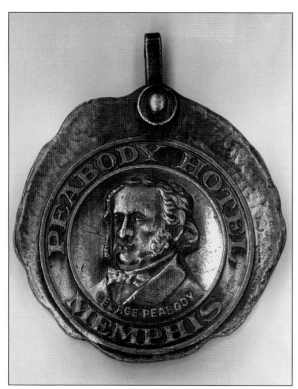

PEABODY KEY FOB. This rare key fob features the image of George Peabody on one side and a depiction of the first Peabody Hotel on the opposite side. It is difficult to date this item. It shows the newer steel addition, which was added after 1906, so that places it after 1906, but before 1925, when the current Peabody Hotel opened.

BALLROOM OR BANQUET HALL. The first Peabody Hotel was, in its day, a social and business center of post-war Memphis. This spacious room would accommodate a large crowd for meetings, dances, banquets, or other social gatherings. The Peabody, like other major hotels of the day, served not only as a social center, with lavish parties and celebrations, but also functioned as a business center. Memphis had fortunately survived much of the destruction visited upon other parts of the South during the Civil War—like Atlanta, Vicksburg, and Columbia, South Carolina, for example—and was therefore ready to move proudly forward into the 20th century. But not quite yet. For, despite its sophistication at many levels, Memphis was, during the immediate post-war years, still a rough and untamed river city. While socially the city possessed the upper classes of the cotton and sugar-based plantation systems, there were also the hard and tough frontiersmen for which Tennessee was noted. Add the large number of ex-Confederates, carpetbaggers, some legitimate Northern businessmen, and the large number of newly freed former slaves, and the mix was eclectic, to say the least. During this period, the Peabody housed traveling salesmen, tradeshows, gamblers, fortune tellers, crooks, card sharks, and hucksters of all kinds. Legend has it that entire plantations were won and lost in card games at the Peabody. And while people of today do not, as a rule, think of hotels when considering funeral arrangements, funerals at hotels were common during this period, and the original Peabody had its share.

DISCOUNT CARD FROM THE FIRST PEABODY, 1898. This discount card entitles the bearer to a discount as stated: " . . . is entitled to a discount of fifty cents a day on the American Plan, on all rooms for which the price is $2.50 per day and upwards, and 25% a day on the European Plan, on all rooms for which the price is $1.00 per day and upwards; and when accompanied by his wife, the price for her shall be the same."

THE PEABODY RESTAURANT. The first Peabody's main restaurant is seen through one of the many surrounding arches.

A Broader View of the Restaurant. Presumably the framed portrait on the far wall is that of George Peabody. Despite hopes to the contrary, the bright promise of the post-war future for Memphis was not to be realized until after the 1870s. During 1873, a yellow fever epidemic devastated the city, with the immediate result that more than half the city's population left altogether. All of the Memphis hotels closed except for the Peabody. There were other problems as well, many of a financial nature, which added to the city's misfortunes. By the end of the decade, however, Memphis had emerged once again, ready to take its place as one of the South's most important cities. The Peabody Hotel, with newly added electric lights and an external iron fire escape, remained the business and social center of Memphis, just as it had since its inception. But trouble for the famed hotel was literally just around the corner.

A Variety of Functions. Here, to the right, are ticket offices for Consolidated and the Illinois Central Railroad. Memphis had always boasted a number of hotels since its earliest days. Joseph Isele in his paper "The History Of Memphis Hotels from 1823 to 1929" mentions that the first hotel in Memphis was the Old Bell Tavern, which was built in 1823 and was located on Front Street. Other hotels quickly followed as the city's population increased from an estimated 50 people in 1820. By 1830, the Clark House was operating at the corner of Main and Winchester. By the early 1840s, Memphis had a half dozen first-class hotels, including the City Hotel, the Exchange Hotel, and the Johnson Hotel. In 1843, according to Isele, the Gayoso House opened and was "one of the most spacious and elegant hotels in the Western Country." By the mid-1850s some of the earlier hotels had disappeared and others had taken their places, among them the United States Hotel, the Apium House, the Arlington, Bostick House, the Commercial House, the Wharf Boat Hotel, the Overton Hotel, and the Washington House, which advertised board and lodging for $1 per day.

THE MEZZANINE LEVEL. The Mezzanine level offered a place for visiting or tables for writing.

INTERIOR VIEW OF THE FIRST HOTEL, PROBABLY MEZZANINE LEVEL. During the 1880s the main hotels in Memphis were the Peabody, the Gaston, the Fransioli, the Clarendon, the Luehrman, and the Duffy. Despite the presence of many hotels in Memphis, the Peabody's chief competitor had always been the Gayoso. The Gayoso opened in February 1843, burned, was rebuilt, reopened in 1858, and again closed on April 2, 1868, prior to the opening of the Peabody in 1869. The Gayoso reopened but succumbed to a fire again on June 28, 1879. By 1896 the Gayoso was in receivership, and was bought in 1898 for $81,000. The Gayoso, like so many hotels of the period, succumbed to fire again on July 4, 1899 in "one of the most spectacular fires of the period." Once again, the Peabody reigned supreme. But the Gayoso was not prepared to be counted out just yet, and another, all-new Gayoso was constructed, which opened in 1902. The Gayoso was again the supreme hotel in the Bluff City.

THE PEABODY AT ITS PRIME. This *c.* 1895 photo shows the first Peabody at its prime as an integral part of the downtown Memphis business district. On January 1, 1906, the Isele Brothers, local hotel owners who had operated the Arlington Hotel, leased the Peabody from its owners at a rental cost of $25,000 per year and took charge of its operation. On July 15, 1906, at 4:30 a.m., part of the Peabody collapsed, destroying 24 rooms as well as the kitchen. As a result of the destruction, the Isele Brothers were released from their lease and an all-new 200-room addition was built at a cost of $350,000. It was the first steel structure erected in Memphis. In 1907 The Memphis Hotel Co. was formed, which owned and operated the hotel.

THE LOBBY. The lobby of the first Peabody Hotel was beautiful and exquisitely detailed.

THE GAYOSO HOTEL. A new Gayoso was constructed in 1902 and was newer and larger than the 1869 Peabody. The new 300-room Gayoso billed itself as "The South's Most Aristocratic Hotel." The population of Memphis had increased rapidly from the slightly more than 20,000 at the end of the Civil War, to around 100,000 by 1900. This was an astounding growth in a mere 35 years. The construction boom, which paralleled this population increase, produced many of Memphis's finest buildings, including some of the South's first skyscrapers. Hotel construction

also soared and within a short span of time, newer, larger, and more magnificent hotels made their debut. The Chisca Hotel opened in 1913 with 400 outside rooms. Outside rooms were certainly desirable in the stagnant summer heat of Memphis. Additionally, the view of the city afforded by outside rooms was desirable, permitting guests with higher level rooms to look out upon the city and the Mississippi River. Like the present Peabody Hotel, and most grand hotels of the time, the Chisca featured an elegant open lobby and mezzanine.

HOTEL CHISCA — MEMPHIS, TENN.

3A-H1125

THE HOTEL CHISCA. The Hotel Chisca, with its "400 bright, outside rooms" and "Homelike Southern Cooking" was one of many newly constructed contenders to hotel dominance in the Bluff City during the early 20th century. Other downtown hotels followed the Chisca in the 1920s. The George Vincent opened at 855 Union. The elegant, 16-story, 400-room, 400-bath Hotel Claridge opened in 1924 at 109 North Main. The Hotel De Voy at 69 Jefferson Street overlooking Confederate Park opened in 1925 before being renamed the King Cotton. The 8-story, 200-room, 200-bath, Hotel Tennessee opened in 1927 at Third and Union, literally across the street from the site of the present Peabody. The magnificent Parkview and William Len Hotel also appeared in Memphis during the years between 1920 and 1930.

THE BALINESE ROOM
The South's most exotic supper club

THE CLARIDGE. The large and elegant 400-room Claridge was built on the site of the former Arlington Hotel in 1922 at a cost of $1,550,000. It opened in 1924 and billed itself as "Memphis's Finest Hotel."

THE HOTEL DE VOY. The Hotel De Voy opened in 1925 overlooking Confederate Park and advertised "safety and comfort without extravagance." Note the highly stylized depiction of Confederate Park in the lower foreground.

HOTEL KING COTTON. The Hotel De Voy was renamed the King Cotton but succumbed to the wrecking ball in the early 1980s and became the site of the new Morgan Keegan building.

Parkview Hotel, Memphis, Tenn

THE PARKVIEW, 1924. The elegant Parkview was one of several grand hotels which opened before the current Peabody. Its location, several miles away from downtown, placed it too far

from the main business district. It changed from hotel to residential hotel, to apartments, and finally to a retirement home.

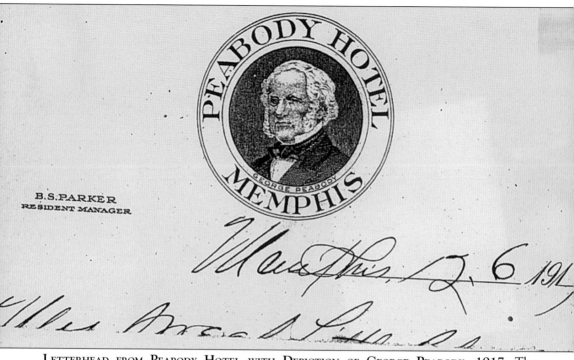

B.S. PARKER
RESIDENT MANAGER

LETTERHEAD FROM PEABODY HOTEL WITH DEPICTION OF GEORGE PEABODY, 1917. The Peabody, which had long served as the city's social and business hub, was not to be outdone by any upstarts. The original structure, however, was inadequate for the elegance and level of service the public had now come to expect, not just from the Peabody, but from hotels in general. In short, the original Peabody could no longer compete with the newer and more modern hotels that Memphis now boasted. Its doors closed for good on August 28, 1923. By fall the same year, construction had started on an all-new Peabody Hotel, to be located at a different site. It would be owned by the Memphis Hotel Co., with former Gayoso manager Albert Parker in charge of the new Peabody construction project. Many architectural plans were submitted, but the final design selected and approved by the board of directors was that of Chicago architect Walter Ahlschlager.

Two

THE ELEGANCE CONTINUES

THE NEW PEABODY HOTEL, C. 1925. This photo depicts the hotel shortly after its opening. The building designed by Ahlschlager was a massive 12-story Italian Renaissance structure with terra cotta exterior detailing and an open 85-by-125-foot, 2-story lobby, which is the center point of the hotel's interior. It was described as follows in a newspaper article from the period: "The decorative scheme of the lobby is 18th century, South Italian. The room rises through two floors with huge square columns supporting the mezzanine balcony. The ceiling is beamed in polychrome and frames two large and very beautiful art glass skylights. A gold railing extends entirely around the mezzanine promenade and the base of it all around has a strip of walnut wood. In the center of the lobby is the fountain, carved out of a block of travertine marble."

THE LOBBY, HOTEL

THE GRANDEST HOTEL IN THE SOUTH. "Summer and winter air-conditioned . . . surrounded by shops and facilities to meet every requirement of the guest." It was at this point that the Peabody undertook measures that would ultimately result in its international status, this largely due to the executive abilities of project head Albert Parker. The preparations for the hotel's construction, staffing, and operation were overseen by Parker, with special attention to detail. He hired Frank Schutt, who had served as assistant manager of the Biltmore Hotel in Atlanta, as the Peabody's first manager. There was no way Parker could have foreseen at the time how significant the hiring of Frank Schutt as the new Peabody Hotel's manager would prove to be to the Peabody's history. In retrospect, it seems to have been one of those rare, almost providential decisions. But Schutt was well qualified for the job, not only personally, but almost genetically. Schutt's great-grandfather had opened a chain of taverns in New York. Schutt's grandfather, J.L.Schutt, built and opened the Laurel House in 1801, the first resort hotel in the Catskills.

ODY, MEMPHIS, TENN.

Schutt's mother's side of the family opened the Catskill Mountain House in 1805. Schutt's father, L.P. Schutt, was manager of the Casa Marina in Key West and associated with the Flagler companies for 30 years. Both of his brothers were also involved in hotel management. The vision for the new Peabody Hotel was that it should offer both elegance and comfort. To that end, all staff members were carefully chosen and trained in the nuances of personal service. As the construction continued, the magnificent one-piece carved marble fountain, which would later hold the famous ducks, was placed in the center of the hotel's ornate lobby, and $500,000 in furniture, a very large sum for 1925, was placed throughout the hotel. Intricately carved wood and plaster were installed on the walls and ceiling of both lobby and mezzanine. In short, everything possible was done to assure that the Peabody would not only be the grandest hotel in Memphis, but in the entire South.

PREVIEW PARTY. The elegant lobby of the new hotel would soon become a gathering place for the city's, and ultimately many of the nation's, elite. With preparations complete, the hotel was set to officially open at 6 a.m. on the morning of September 2, 1925. But on the previous evening, September 1, a fabulous preview party was held for a private guest list consisting of 1,200 notables. The invitation to this gala event featured a picture of the new Hotel Peabody as it was then known under which were printed the words "The South's Finest— One Of America's Best."

GRAND OPENING INVITATION. This invitation was extended to special guests for the grand opening of the new hotel.

GRAND OPENING INVITATION. The inside page of the grand opening invitation listed the officers, directors, and other officials of the new hotel.

PROGRAM MENU. The opening festivities offered a dedication, a seated dinner with speech, and dancing in the ballroom. Those in attendance at this gala preview party were treated to a magnificent dinner and a night of dancing, live music, and revelry. The hotel's staff of 450 worked through the night and were ready and still on duty when the hotel officially opened the next morning as scheduled.

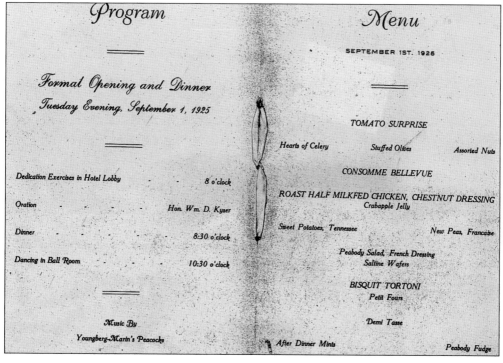

Memphis Hotel Company

Officers and Directors

William Parker Halliday _Memphis_	President
Stuyvesant Fish _New York City_	Vice President
Albert Luman Parker _Memphis_	Vice President
John Price Edrington _Memphis_	Secretary-Treasurer

Directors

Hugh R. Wynne
Memphis

Jacob Goldsmith
Memphis

Henry T. Bunn
Memphis

Simon J. Shwartz
New Orleans

Paul H. Saunders
New Orleans

A. L. Parker _In Charge of Construction, Equipment and Operation_	Vice Pres't & Gen. Mgr.
F. R. Schutt _Memphis_	Resident Manager
Walter W. Ahlschlager, Inc., _Chicago_	Architects
Thos. H. Allen _Memphis_	Mechanical Engineer
McKellar, Kyser & Allen _Memphis_	Attorneys
Marx & Bensdorf _Memphis_	Rental Agents

Program

Formal Opening and Dinner
Tuesday Evening, September 1, 1925

Dedication Exercises in Hotel Lobby	8 o'clock
Oration	Hon. Wm. D. Kyser
Dinner	8:30 o'clock
Dancing in Ball Room	10:30 o'clock

Music By
Youngberg-Marin's Peacocks

Menu

SEPTEMBER 1ST. 1925

TOMATO SURPRISE

Hearts of Celery   Stuffed Olives   Assorted Nuts

CONSOMME BELLEVUE

ROAST HALF MILKFED CHICKEN, CHESTNUT DRESSING
Crabapple Jelly

Sweet Potatoes, Tennessee   New Peas, Francaise

Peabody Salad, French Dressing
Saltine Wafers

BISQUIT TORTONI
Petit Fours

Demi Tasse

After Dinner Mints   Peabody Fudge

PEABODY BELL BOY STAFF. These employees posed for a photo near the hotel's entrance.

ELEVATOR LOBBY. The elevator lobby was uncluttered and elegant.

LOBBY SHOPS AND OFFICES. Those familiar with older hotels in major cities will remember that it was once common practice for merchants of all types to have offices and shops in hotels, usually on the mezzanine and main levels, with some even located below the main floor. This tradition, abandoned largely in the 1960s, has again come into vogue. Between the 1920s and 1960s the Peabody featured more than 40 shops and offices of various types positioned around the lobby and mezzanine areas, although all of the original business spaces were not fully occupied until 1934.

COVER OF *HI-LITES*. During the late 1920s, and possibly beyond, the hotel published its own weekly in-house magazine, *Hi-Lites*, which detailed upcoming events at the hotel, provided information of local interest to guests such as theatre and train schedules, a hotel directory, and featured advertisements from some of the merchants located at the Peabody.

HOTEL PEABODY STAFF

MR. A. L. PARKER, *Pres. & General Mgr.*   MR. F. R. SCHUTT, *Mgr.*
Miss Mary Pelham, *Manager's Secretary*

It is gratifying to see patrons and guests of the Hotel Peabody daily knowing and recognizing the staff of the Hotel. It is the wish of Mr. Schutt, the manager, that you become better acquainted; his assistants are always glad to serve you. Do not hesitate to call upon them.

R. D. BEMISS	First Assistant Manager
ARTHUR SCHOEMBS	Assistant Manager—Purchases
LOUIS WEIL	Assistant Manager
T. J. McGINN	Assistant Manager
W. P. HALLIDAY, JR.	Assistant Manager
ROY FARROW	Night Manager
ERNEST VOLLRATH	Maitre d'Hotel
GILBERT BLANC	Chef-Steward
ALEX GUIGOU	Grill Manager

Mrs. Marie McLendon   *Social Secretary*

J. B. Lindsay	General Auditor	H. O. Gardner, Geo. Prenzel	Room Clerks
H. M. Wisotzkey	General Auditor	Misses Ruth Lipsey, Tempe Wills	Cashiers
Miss Gertrude L. Perce	Auditor	Miss Alma Perry, Mrs. Martha Smith	Secs.
		Lillian Vanpool, Cherry Wilcox	Bill Clerks
Miss Mary Walsh	Housekeeper	W. H. Caldwell	Night Clerk
C. H. Stanton	Chief Engineer	E. W. Atwood, E. Hoeffer	Information
Mrs. Nell McIntyre	Tea Room	E. A. Campbell, Bob White	Mail Clerks
H. Toscano	Pastry Chef	J. R. Cooper	House Carpenter
Mrs. E. B. Frayser	Catering	J. W. Dicky	Laundry
Joe H. Roulhac	Mgr. Printing Dept.	R. S. Barrett	Time Keeper
Mrs. Bernice Hurdle	Telephone Supervisor	Miss Nell DeZonia	Public Stenographer
Miss May Baldridge	Supt. Cigar Dept.		
Blue Steele	Musical Director	Head Waiter	W. Alonzo Locke
L. S. Loyd	Valet Service	Head Porter	Jack Powell
Miss Berniece Fort	General Cashier	Chief Bell Captain	W. P. Snelson

Press of Memphis Hotel Co.

HI-LITES   At Hotel Peabody
Memphis, Tenn.

VOL. I   MARCH 11, 1928   NO. V

A weekly magazine published in the interest of the social life of Hotel Peabody, the South's most beautiful hotel. Distributed in each room of the Peabody and to the favored folks who it is our privilege to serve.

Marie McLendon, *Editor*

A. L. PARKER, *President*
F. R. SCHUTT, *Manager*

CONTENTS

[1]

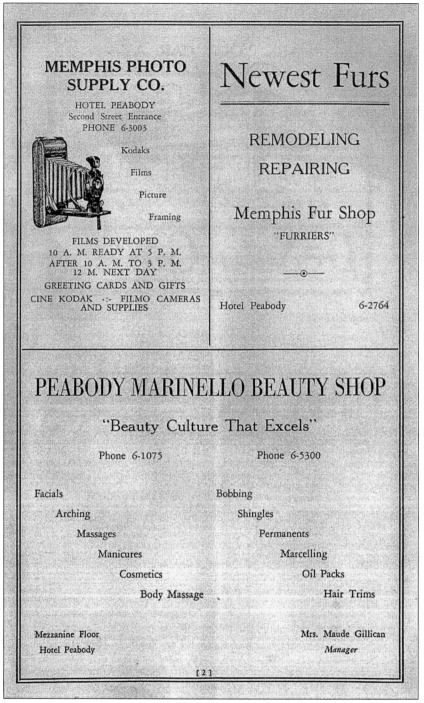
PEABODY ADVERTISEMENTS. Businesses of all types called the Peabody home.

OLD-FASHIONED SHOE SHINES. Before the days of athletic shoes, many hotels had in-house shoe shops and shoe-shine stands. Guests could leave shoes to be polished and have them delivered to their rooms.

MORE PEABODY ADVERTISEMENTS. Coffee was as important in the past as it is now.

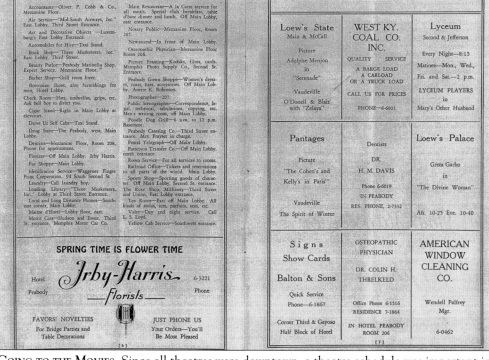

GOING TO THE MOVIES. Since all theatres were downtown, a theatre schedule was important in the days before television.

TRAINS ARRIVING AT AND DEPARTING FROM GRAND CENTRAL STATION
Corner Main St. and Calhoun Ave., Memphis, Tennessee
Ticket Office operated by Hotel Peabody in Hotel Lobby   J. G. McKinnon, *Manager*
Corrected to February 26, 1928—Central Standard Time

ILLINOIS CENTRAL

Train No. ARRIVES		Train No. DEPARTS	
7 Panama Limited	12:31 a.m.	7 Panama Limited	12:36 a.m.
2 From New Orleans, Jackson	6:35 a.m.	2 For Chicago, St. Louis & Louisville	6:50 a.m.
15 The Chickasaw	7:30 a.m.	126 Fulton Local	7:50 a.m.
3 From Chicago	8:15 a.m.	133 Grenada Local	8:15 a.m.
103 From Cincinnati, Louisville, St. Louis	8:20 a.m.	3 For Jackson & New Orleans	9:10 a.m.
132 Grenada Local	9:00 a.m.	110 For Chicago, St Louis	4:35 p.m.
133 Fulton Local	9:10 a.m.	131 Grenada Local	5:00 p.m.
134 Grenada Local	4:30 p.m.	4 For Chicago	7:35 p.m.
125 Fulton Local	6:40 p.m.	104 For Louisville & Cincinnati	9:10 p.m.
4 From New Orleans, Jackson	6:55 p.m.	8 For St. Louis & Chicago (Sleeping car only)	9:05 p.m.
8 From New Orleans	9:00 p.m.	16 The Chickasaw	11:20 p.m.
1 From Chicago, St. Louis and Louisville	11:25 p.m.	1 For Jackson, New Orleans	11:50 p.m.

FRISCO LINES

	ARRIVES		DEPARTS
805 Memphian	7:05 a.m.	921 Birmingham Local	7:10 a.m.
108 Sunnyland	7:20 a.m.	108 Sunnyland to Kansas City	7:45 a.m.
105 Kansas City-Florida Special	7:45 a.m.	808 Sunnyland to St. Louis	8:00 a.m.
924 From Mobile and Aberdeen	8:30 a.m.	105 Kansas City-Florida Special	8:05 a.m.
922 Birmingham Local	5:50 p.m.	802 St. Louis Express	9:00 a.m.
103 Kansas City Express	6:55 p.m.	104 Kansas City Express	9:15 a.m.
801 St. Louis Express	6:35 p.m.	923 For Aberdeen and Mobile	5:30 p.m.
106 Kansas City-Florida Special	7:20 p.m.	106 Kansas City-Florida Special	7:45 p.m.
807 Sunnyland from St. Louis	8:45 p.m.	107 Sunnyland	9:35 p.m.
107 Sunnyland from Colorado & Kansas City	9:15 p.m.	806 Memphian	11:20 p.m.

CHICAGO, ROCK ISLAND & PACIFIC RAILROAD

	ARRIVES		DEPARTS
112 Memphis-Californian	6:40 a.m.	49 Hot Springs-Panama Limited	12:45 a.m.
42 Choctaw Limited	12:45 p.m.	603 Little Rock Passenger	7:00 a.m.
604 Passenger	4:55 p.m.	45 Hot Springs Limited	8:30 a.m.
46 Hot Springs Limited	6:55 p.m.	41 Choctaw Limited	2:30 p.m.
50 Hot Springs-Panama Limited	9:00 p.m.	111 Californian	9:05 p.m.

YAZOO & MISSISSIPPI VALLEY RAILROAD

	ARRIVES		DEPARTS
12 Northern Express	6:25 a.m.	21 Traveler's Special	1:15 a.m.
32 Tutwiler & Lambert	10:20 a.m.	23 Delta Express	8:40 a.m.
30 G'ville, G'wood, Clarksdale	10:30 a.m.	31 Yazoo City-Tutwiler	9:05 a.m.
24 Vicksburg & Clarksdale	4:10 p.m.	33 Lambert & Tutwiler	3:30 p.m.
34 Yazoo City-Tutwiler	4:25 p.m.	39 C'dale, Tutwiler, G'wood	4:00 p.m.
26 C'land, G'ville & Clarksdale	7:00 p.m.	15 Southern Express	5:00 p.m.

All Trains run daily, including Sunday, unless otherwise specified
Note changes in Illinois Central Trains

MEMPHIS UNION STATION TIME TABLE NO. 109
Corrected to February 12, 1928—Central Standard Time

L. & N. R. R. ARRIVING

			L. & N. R. R. DEPARTURE	
†127 From Humboldt	7:57 a.m.	*110 For Paris	8:10 a.m.
*101 From Louisville, Cincinnati	8:10 a.m.	*198 "The Pan-American"	7:40 a.m.
*103 From Louisville, Cincinnati	3:25 p.m.	*102 For Louisville, Cincinnati	12:55 p.m.
*109 From Paris	8:25 p.m.	†128 For Humboldt	5:45 p.m.
*199 "The Pan-American"	10:05 p.m.	*104 For Louisville, Cincinnati	8:45 p.m.

SOUTHERN RAILROAD

	ARRIVING	SOUTHERN RAILROAD DEPARTURE	
* 25 From Washington	6:50 a.m.	* 36 For Chattanooga	8:10 a.m.
* 7 From Sommerville	7:30 a.m.	* 12 For Sheffield	4:15 p.m.
* 11 From Sheffield	10:30 a.m.	* 8 For Sommerville	6:00 p.m.
* 35 From Chattanooga	6:40 p.m.	* 26 For Washington	8:10 p.m.

N., C. & ST. L. RY.

	ARRIVING	N., C. & ST. L. RY. DEPARTURE	
*102 From Nashville	7:00 a.m.	*105 For Nashville	7:30 a.m.
* 10 From Jackson	8:40 a.m.	*103 For Nashville	1:15 p.m.
*104 From Nashville	3:15 p.m.	* 9 For Jackson	5:10 p.m.
*106 From Nashville	9:50 p.m.	*101 For Nashville	11:59 p.m.

MISSOURI PACIFIC R. R.

	ARRIVING	MISSOURI PACIFIC R. R. DEPARTURE	
*330 From Helena	9:45 a.m.	*239 For Newport	5:30 a.m.
*224 "The Tennessean"	7:30 a.m.	*335 For Helena, McGehee, La.	9:00 a.m.
*202 "Sunshine Special"	7:00 a.m.	*219 For Hot Springs	9:30 a.m.
*204 From Texas	12:50 p.m.	*225 "The Texan"	6:50 p.m.
*220 From Hot Springs	6:50 p.m.	*203 For Texas	2:15 p.m.
*236 From Bald Knob	9:30 a.m.	*223 "The Tennessean"	11:20 p.m.
*334 From Helena, McGehee & La.	6:15 p.m.	*331 To Helena	7:00 p.m.
*238 From Newport	10:00 p.m.	*201 "Sunshine Special"	11:25 p.m.

COTTON BELT ROUTE
ST. L. S. W. RY.

	ARRIVING	COTTON BELT ROUTE ST. L. S. W. RY. DEPARTURE	
* 2 From Arkansas and Texas	6:50 p.m.	* 1 For Arkansas & Texas	11:20 a.m.
* 12 "Lone Star Limited"	7:10 a.m.	* 11 "Lone Star Limited"	11:00 p.m.

Note changes in L & N & Mo. Pac. Trains

*Daily   †Daily except Sunday
J. H. MOORE, Station Master

[20]

TRAIN SCHEDULE. Like most major cities of the era, Memphis was a significant railroad center. This 1928 schedule of arriving and departing trains provides an example.

TRAVEL AGENCY. One of the many businesses operating within the Peabody was the Peabody's own Peabody Steamship and Tourist Agency. This agency opened at the same time as the hotel, in 1925, and conducted tours and made detailed travel arrangements. A newspaper article from the 1930s described its services as follows: "No matter what ship the traveler desires to make his crossing on, no matter what Parisian cafe he wishes to visit for a carefree half-hour, no matter what size camel he wants for his pilgrimage to the Pyramids, the Hotel Peabody Steamship and Tourist Agency has the arrangements within its scope. The traveler who leaves his itinerary and comfort in their hands has no worries."

All Milk, Cream, Butter and

Garden Products used at the Hotel

are from our

GAYOSO FARMS

HORN LAKE, MISSISSIPPI

The Gayoso Farms of 684 Acres, located at Horn Lake, Mississippi, fourteen miles south of Hotel Peabody on the Memphis-Hernando Road, are owned and operated by the Memphis Hotel Company for the purpose of furnishing its hotels in Memphis (The Peabody, Gayoso and Chisca) with "Golden Yellow" Guernsey Milk and Cream, "Leading in Quality" Hampshire meat and orchard and garden products—indicative of the high standard of service it has established and maintains.

For years a definite breeding program has been carried on in both the Guernsey and Hampshire Departments. Through careful selection, skillful mating—using best sires, and proper care and feeding, both the herds have been developed to first rank in their respective breeds in the South, and among the first in the United States.

Gayoso's Roberta's Actor

[19]

ADVERTISEMENT. This advertisement from *Hi-Lites* promoting Gayoso Farms was meant to inform hotel guests that the meat and dairy products served in the Peabody, as well as in The Gayoso and Chisca Hotels, were of the highest quality obtainable, as indeed they were. The Peabody Hotel opened under the auspices of the Memphis Hotel Co., which, at the time, owned all three of Memphis's most important downtown hotels.

PEABODY BARBERSHOP. Every hotel of the period had a barbershop and the Peabody's was the finest available. Note the manicure table at the far end of the room.

ATTENTION TO DETAIL. The women's beauty shop also featured manicure tables.

Despite the opening of and competition from other significant hotels of the period, notably the Claridge, Parkview, King Cotton, and the Tennessee, the Peabody almost immediately established itself as Memphis's and the Mid-South's premier hotel, a title it retains. Several elements have combined, along with the passage of time, to earn the Peabody this unique reputation. First and foremost was the hotel's dedication to the comfort of its guests. Staff members prided themselves on remembering the names of the hotel's many patrons. This attention to detail only added to its reputation for the best in both food and service. One example involves the hotel's gift packs. A *Press-Scimitar* article from 1952 mentioned that guests with advance reservations at the hotel found in their rooms small packages with their names printed in gold. Inside the packages were complimentary items tailored for either a man or woman guest, or both. Items included deodorant, shaving cream, hair tonic, lipstick, toothpaste, shampoo, and other items. Today, most hotels and motels provide shampoo and hair conditioner, or skin lotion, but this was rare in the early 1950s and the Peabody was one of only 250 hotels in North America to provide this service.

THE SODA SHOP AND THE NITE CAP CLUB. The soda shop offered toiletry items, cigars, coffee, milkshakes, ice cream, and Coca-Cola, considered by many in Dixie to be the fabled "Nectar of the Gods." Another grand tradition began with the opening of the new Peabody Hotel—the tradition of being the premier location for some of the best live music in the South. Within a year of opening, the new hotel had Friday night dining and dancing in a private club called the Nite Cap Club, which was started by a group of locals in the hotel's former Italian Room. The top bands and orchestras of the day regularly played in one or the other of the hotel's many ballrooms. Among the favorites of the era were George Hamilton, Blue Steele, Oswald Lobrecue, and Carlos Molina.

You are cordially invited to become
a member of the

• NITE • CAP • CLUB •

meeting every Friday evening
NOVEMBER through APRIL
10 p. m. to 2 a. m.

COVER CHARGE
includes souvenir
for the lady
$3.00 PER COUPLE
$2.00 SINGLE

ENTERTAINMENT
by Seymour Simon and his
Hotel Peabody Orchestra
FEATURING:
Miss Dorothy Page
Mr. "Doc" Davis

OPENING DATE -- Friday, November Fourth
Admission By Enclosed Card

ASON 1932 & 19__

THE LADIES' SHOP. The ladies' shop sold purses, handbags, linens, jewelry, and dresses.

LLOYD'S LIQUOR STORE. This store was located in the Peabody. Its art deco lines are clearly discernible in this photograph from 1940.

THE BILLIARD ROOM. The room shown here was probably located in the basement.

A CORNER ROOM. Note the large steam-powered radiator that provided heat in the winter months. The windows were functional and provided both ventilation and cooling in the summer.

A Larger Corner Suite. Corner rooms provided much-needed cross-ventilation.

What really made the Peabody famous in terms of entertainment were its concerts on the roof. Hotel rooftop concerts were not uncommon during the pre-World War II era at large hotels in places like Miami, and other large Southern cities. Even Memphis had rooftop dances and concerts at the Magnolia Roof Gardens at the Hotel Claridge. And yet, it was the rooftop concerts and dances at the Peabody that became most famous. This tradition started as early as 1926, less than a year after the new hotel opened. The first outdoor roof garden was called the Owl's Nest. An article in the *Commercial Appeal* described the opening evening's festivities:

> All of Society turned out last night for the first try at the new roof garden, the Owl's Nest, which lies atop Hotel Peabody. Under the light of the big full moon, some 500 of the city's elite gathered to spend a delightful evening dining, dancing and enjoying a program of cabaret numbers. The spacious roof of the hotel has been transformed into an outdoor garden, with iron tables, striped awnings and two large dance floors. The Seven Aces orchestra provided music for as many as cared to Charleston or waltz in the cool breeze. Judging from the opening night of the garden, it will be the gathering place of society during the long summer months.

THE SKYWAY. This open part of the roof served as a dance area before later being enclosed as "The Skyway." Nationally prominent acts of the day, including Jan Garber, Paul Whiteman, Ray Anthony, Ted Weems, Les Brown, Benny Goodman, Harry James, Lawrence Welk, Ozzie Nelson, Dorothy Lamour, Snooky Lanson, and other top names frequently played concerts for dancing under the stars. For a time in fact, CBS broadcast concerts live on the radio from the roof. There is nothing like being on the roof of the Peabody Hotel on a warm summer night.

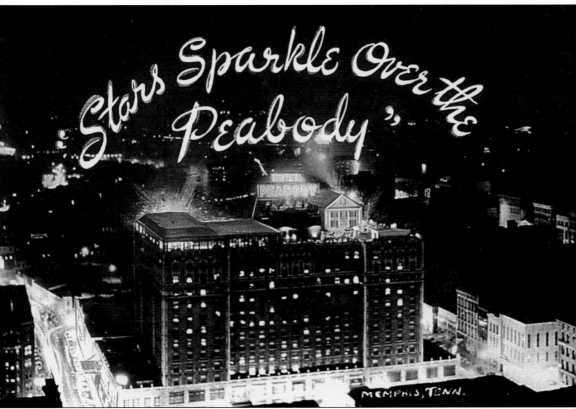

THE PLANTATION ROOF. Throughout the early years, the name of the Peabody's roof changed several times. It was alternately called the Moroccan Roof, the Marine Roof, and finally, in 1938, became known as The Plantation Roof, a name that stuck. This was due to the construction of a Southern mansion facade on top of the roof, a structure that remains to this day. The Plantation Roof was originally intended to be named the Tara Roof after Scarlett O'Hara's house in *Gone With The Wind*, but the name Plantation Roof had the same connotation without any potential legal entanglements. This vintage period postcard shows the Plantation Roof at night prior to the creation of the enclosed skyway.

THE PLANTATION ROOF ON A SUMMER NIGHT. It doesn't get any better. But Memphis does get cold in the winter. The popularity of the profitable rooftop concerts needed to be extended beyond the warmer weather. In 1938, Frank Schutt, the same hotel manager responsible for the Peabody Ducks, was given approval by the hotel's board of directors to create a covered circular ballroom on the top floor of the hotel. Architects George Mahan and Nowland Van Powell were selected as designers, and Fred Young and Sam Maury were selected as general contractors. The project was formally announced in October 1938. This new, round facility would feature removable floor-to-ceiling windows, as well as raised seating, similar to that found in major Las Vegas showrooms. Popular rooftop dancing would be improved with a new 2,000-square-foot circular beechwood dance floor with a 64-foot diameter. It was felt that a unique facility of this type would allow the hotel to provide big name entertainment year-round. Additionally, the new room would be an excellent location for large social events of all types, having nearly twice the capacity of the downstairs ballroom, and provide even more revenues for the hotel. The plan was approved and the construction undertaken with a final cost expected to be in excess of

$100,000. Several names had been suggested, including the Regency Room, Aurora Terrace, the Rainbow Room, and Garden of the Moon, although at the time of the announcement no name had been chosen. It was, despite its modernistic "swank" design, a major construction project. Over 90 tons of steel had to be transported to the top of the hotel through temporary outside elevators. When the project was completed, a grand opening celebration was held and 1,200 revelers attended the opening festivities, tickets for which were sold out weeks in advance. Henry King and his orchestra provided the entertainment and a magnificent lobster feast was served at midnight. The new showroom situated on top of the hotel was aptly named "the Skyway" and was the equal of any in the nation. The domed circular ceiling was painted midnight blue and punctuated with recessed lights, giving the impression of being under a night sky. While the new room occupied a substantial part of the roof area formerly used for concerts and dancing, more than enough of the original area still remained for parties and dancing in an outside area on the roof.

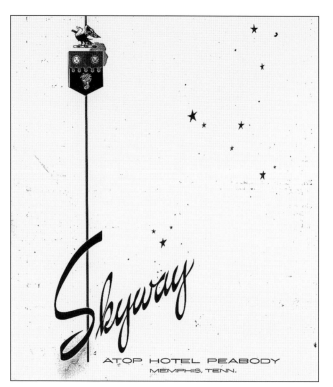

Skyway

ATOP HOTEL PEABODY
MEMPHIS, TENN.

Skyway Menu. These two menu pages give some indication of the type and variety of food items available, and are indicative of how the Peabody developed such a great reputation for wonderful food.

HORS D'OEUVRES - POTAGES

Fresh Gulf Shrimp, Remoulade 1.00	**Lump Crabmeat Ravigotte** 1.00	**Chilled Tomato Juice** 30
with a famous sauce made of creole mustard and horseradish or cocktail sauce.	served with a creamy white sauce made with pimentos, green pepper, English mustard.	**Old-Fashioned Vegetable Soup** 40
Onion Soup au Gratin 50	**Fresh Assorted Fruit Cocktail Supreme** 70	**Fresh Cream of Tomato Soup** 40
made from an old French recipe topped with cheese and croutons.		
Chilled Tomato Bouillon 30	**Split Pea Soup, Croutons** 35	**Stuffed Celery with Blue Cheese** 85
Fresh Orange Juice 50	**Assorted Canapes** 75	

ENTREES

Flaming Shishkabob 3.50
chunks of choice tenderloin, slices of tomato, onion and pepper, fresh mushrooms broiled on a sword and served aflame. French fries.

Filet Mignon 4.50
an 8 ounce aged cut of tenderloin served with fresh mushrooms, French fries.

French Cut Double Lamb Chops Mirabeau 4.25
with the zest of charcoal flavor. Served with tomato and mint jelly.

Chateaubriand (1 lb.), Garni with Bearnaise Sauce 9.00
a juicy cut of beef tenderloin, aged and good, prepared by Chef Mason. Served with fresh vegetables this is a real treat for two.

U. S. Choice 12 Ounce Sirloin Steak, Maitre d'Hotel 5.25
a great cut of beef, charcoal smoked. Served with potato, butter and fresh watercress.

Rock Cornish Game Hen 3.25
the delicate flavor of this game and the tender white meat accompanied by pecan dressing and orange sauce would please a King. (30-45 minutes.)

Grilled Sugar-Cured Ham Steak 2.75
broiled Pineapple and French fried potatoes.

Roast Prime Ribs of Beef au jus 3.65
cooked the English way with heavy salt and served with a giant baked potato with sour cream, chives and bacon chips. Tossed dinner salad.

Lobster Thermidor 4.50
fresh from Maine, the tender meat of this lobster is blended with fresh mushrooms to make this a true Memphis treat. Julienne potatoes.

Fried Half Spring Chicken 2.25
fried the Southern way and served with a spiced peach, honey and corn fritters.

Chopped Beef Tenderloin Tips 2.25
juicy tenderloin tips, ground, then cooked to your desire and served with stuffed onion.

Broiled Fresh Brook Trout (2) 3.50
with almandine butter and tartare sauce. Baked potato or French fries.

Peabody Jr. Special 6 oz. Sirloin 3.50
charcoal broiled to your order with baked or French fried potatoes.

Fried Louisiana Jumbo Shrimp 2.85
Served with Julienne potatoes, fried onion rings and Tartare sauce.

Breaded Veal Cutlet 2.50
spaghetti milanaise.

——— THE ABOVE ENTREES INCLUDE ROLLS AND BUTTER, COFFEE OR TEA ———

Fresh Vegetables may be substituted for Potatoes on above orders

DINNER GUESTS REMAINING AFTER 8 P.M. ARE SUBJECT TO 20% FEDERAL TAX ON ALL ITEMS
Guests Served Dinner Before 9 P.M. May Remain for Dancing, Except Friday and Saturday Without Cover Charge

We Will Be Pleased to Serve You Any Items Not Listed at a la Carte Prices.

BEVERAGES

Cafe, pot 30	**Tea, hot or chilled** 25	**Milk or Buttermilk** 25

SKYWAY MENU AND POSTCARD. The Skyway, which opened on January 1, 1939, looks much the same today as it did when the postcard below was made in the 1940s.

SALADES

Peabody Fruit Plate 1.75	Chef's Cotton King Salad Bowl 1.50
created especially for the Skyway Room — a Summertime surprise.	lettuce, romaine, watercress tossed together and topped with chopped eggs, julienne of ham and turkey, anchovy, oil and vinegar.
Watercress Salad ...... .65	
with chopped hard boiled eggs and a tangy Blue Cheese dressing.	Head Lettuce ...... .35
Louisiana Shrimp Salad Plate 1.50	with 1000 Island or French dressing. Blue Cheese dressing 25c extra.
Hearts of Lettuce and Tomato ...... .50	Crisp Tossed Dinner Salad ...... .35
your favorite dressing, bacon chips.	with 1000 Island or French dressing. Blue Cheese dressing 25c extra.

A LA CARTE

Cheese or Mushroom Omelette 1.25	
Eggs Benedict 1.50	
broiled ham and poached eggs on crisp toast. Hollandaise sauce.	
Peabody Club Sandwich 1.25	
slices of turkey, crisp bacon, lettuce and tomato served with potato chips.	
Grilled Ham Steak 2.25	
with eggs.	
Turkey and Ham au Gratin 2.00	
with julienne potatoes.	

LEGUMES

Stuffed Onions ...... .35	
French Fried Potatoes ...... .30	
Asparagus Spears, Butter ...... .60	
String Beans Almandine ...... .35	
Fresh Corn on the Cob ...... .35	
Broccoli au Beurre ...... .35	
Potatoes au Gratin ...... .40	
Baked Potato ...... .40	
filled with butter, chives and bacon.	

DESSERTS

Crepes Suzette 1.00	Peach Melba ...... .50
prepared at your table and set aflame.	created for the famous singer Melba by the great chef A. Escoffier. This dessert has been a gourmet's delight for years. A whole peach, stuffed with ice cream topped with the famous Melba sauce and sprinkled with toasted almonds.
Strawberry Romanoff 1.00	
Skyway Ice Box Pies ...... .35	
blackbottom, coconut and lemon. Graham cracker crust.	Alaska Flambe ...... .75
Fruit Sherbets ...... .35	Ice Cream ...... .30
Creme de Menthe, Strawberry or	Vanilla, Chocolate or Strawberry served with Petits Fours.
Chocolate Parfait ...... .40	
Coupe de St. Jacques ...... .60	Eclair Eugene 1.00
when Brother John was sleeping he dreamed of this dessert: a macedoine of six fresh fruits marinated in fine brandy, topped with three scoops of assorted ices.	the shell is filled with vanilla ice cream and covered with a fabulous sauce made at your table —chocolate, creme de cacao and fine brandy.
Charlotte Russe ...... .40	Cherries Jubilee 1.00
Bavarian Cream au Sherry, decorated with lady fingers and topped with whipped cream.	ice cream and black bing cherries flamed at your table.

FRENCH PASTRY TRAY
30c
Make your own selections from this beautiful assortment of
"PASTRIES BY OTTO"

SKYWAY BUFFET
EVERY THURSDAY NITE — 7 P.M. TO MIDNIGHT
$4.00 PER PERSON
(Includes buffet dinner, set-ups, cover charge and tax)

— ALL ITEMS SERVED UNTIL HALF PAST MIDNIGHT —

THE SKYWAY, HOTEL PEABODY, MEMPHIS, TENN.

THE SKYWAY. The Skyway became the favorite spot in Memphis for large meetings and luncheons, as well as for indoor dancing and dining.

THE SKYWAY ATOP HOTEL PEABODY—MEMPHIS, TENNESSEE. This somewhat imaginative Skyway menu cover accurately conveys the spirit of a night of dancing at the Skyway.

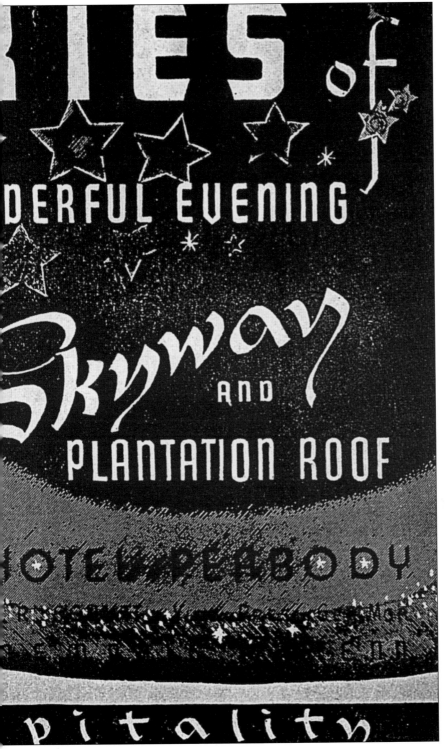

PHOTO COVER. A strolling photographer took pictures which could be purchased by the patrons of the Skyway and the Plantation Roof. When the photos were processed, they arrived inside this attractive cover which came in a variety of colors.

PEABODY MEMORABILIA. These World War II-era photographs of people enjoying the Skyway came from the Peabody's Memorabilia Room on the Mezzanine level. They are just a small sampling of the photographs on hand. Additionally there are letters, menus, china, silverware, glasses, postcards, and other souvenirs of the hotel's long history. A recorded message leads the visitor through the interesting history of the hotel.

ROOFTOP DINING. Dinner on the Plantation Roof has long been a Memphis tradition.

DINNER IN THE SKYWAY.

DINING ON THE PLANTATION ROOF.

Mr. and Mrs. Jack Belz. Pictured are Mrs. Jack Belz, third from left, and Jack Belz, third from right, second row. It's doubtful that when this picture was made that Jack Belz had even the slightest idea that he would someday become such a significant part of the Peabody's history.

SOUTHERN AIR SERVICE, INC.

REQUESTS YOUR PRESENCE

AT

DAWN PATROL BANQUET AND DANCE

GEORGIAN ROOM

HOTEL PEABODY

MONDAY EVENING, DECEMBER TWENTIETH

NINETEEN HUNDRED AND THIRTY-SEVEN

7 P.M.

INFORMAL
R. S. V. P.

GUEST RESERVATION
ON REQUEST

DAWN PATROL BANQUET AND DANCE. An invitation from Southern Air Service is typical of the hotel's pre-war activities.

A RARE SURVIVING LUGGAGE TAG. The slogan "The South's Finest, One of America's Best" appears on the tag.

Musical Programme

BY

Smith Ballew

nd His Hotel Peabody Orchestra

SMITH BALLEW — Director

ginia Franck, Vocalist   Marshall Smith, Vocalist

"FOURSOME"

rshall Smith — Bill Barford — Ray Johnson — Dell Porter

Violins: Alexander Peck, first; Charles Riley, second; Bill ford, third; Ray Johnson, fourth.

Saxophones: Edwin Scherr, first; Lil Koch, second; Dell Por-, third.

Piano, Chalmers McGregor; drums, Ray McKinley, bass, Har- Goodman; trombone, A. Glenn Miller; cornet, J. D. Wade.

PROGRAMME

"Bolero" — Ravel

Tone Poem — Raymond Johnson
String Quartet

"More Than You Know" — Vincent Youman
The Foursome and Mr. Ballew

"Blue Hours" — Wayne King

The Foursome — Popular Requests

SPECIAL CONCERT DINNE

Served from 6:00 to 8:30 p.m.

$1.50 PER PERSON

Served to One Person Only

———

Oyster Cocktail on Half Shell or
Fresh Fruit Cocktail, Florida

———

Olives   Ce

———

Cream of Fresh Tomato au Croutons
Consomme Madrilaine

———

Broiled Jumbo Whitefish, Maitre d'Hotel
Minute Steak Saute, Bordelaise
Breast of Capon, Under Bell, Eugenie
Roast Tennessee Turkey, Cranberry Sauce

———

Louisiana Sweet Potatoes
New Potatoes Brioche   New Cauliflower, Hollan
Green Peas Bonnefemme

———

Fan Salad, French Dressing

———

Choice of
Fig Pudding with Custard Sauce
Lemon Chiffon Pie   Minc
Two-Tone Brick Ice Cream with Petit Fours
Assorted French Pastry   Frozen

———

Coffee,   Tea,   Milk   or   Buttermilk

HOTEL PEABODY   DEC. 10, 19

Memphis - Tenn;

1933 Invitation. This "Special Concert Dinner" looks like it was great fun. The menu was inviting and so was the entertainment. Note the name of trombonist, "A. Glenn Miller," who would eventually become the most successful and famous band leader of his time. Many famous people, as well as those who would later become famous, played the Peabody. Screen star Dorothy Lamour had a special connection to the Peabody. While participating in a talent contest she was spotted by Peabody band leader Herbie Kay, who happened to be in the audience. Introduced as "Miss New Orleans of 1931," the dark-haired beauty so charmed Mr. Kay that he hired her to sing with the Peabody Orchestra at the Skyway. From there she went on to sing with Rudy Vallee, and became the first vocalist to sing at New York City's famed Stork Club. Her singing led to her career as an actress. She starred in the 1940 classic, *The Road to Singapore*, the first of the great Bob Hope and Bing Crosby "Road Series" films. Dorothy Lamour enjoyed a long and successful career in Hollywood and made nearly 50 movies.

HOTEL PEABODY

(An Alsonett Hotel)

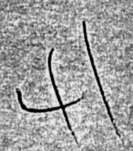

Your Waiter Number Is

"YOUR WAITER NUMBER IS." This card was most likely placed on banquet tables for special occasions. The first Cotton Carnival, a three-day long Mardi Gras-type festival with an Old South theme, took place in March 1931 as part of a plan to raise the spirits of Memphians during the Depression. It started an annual tradition that would continue through the early 1980s. As time passed, the Cotton Carnival became the most eagerly awaited Memphis social event of the year. The festival expanded from three days to a week, and due to weather conditions, moved from March to May. Krewes were organized for Cotton Carnival as with New Orleans Mardi Gras. As time passed and the festival continued to grow, the Peabody Hotel served as a command center for much of this celebration of cotton, and an eagerly anticipated grand ball was held on the roof of the hotel every year.

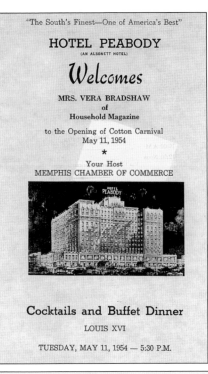

"The South's Finest—One of America's Best"

HOTEL PEABODY
(AN ALSONETT HOTEL)

Welcomes

MRS. VERA BRADSHAW
of
Household Magazine

to the Opening of Cotton Carnival
May 11, 1954

★

Your Host
MEMPHIS CHAMBER OF COMMERCE

Cocktails and Buffet Dinner

LOUIS XVI

TUESDAY, MAY 11, 1954 — 5:30 P.M.

COTTON CARNIVAL INVITATION. This May 1954 invitation welcomes attendees to the opening of that year's Cotton Carnival.

COTTON CARNIVAL MENU. The itinerary is included as well as an appealing menu. What is most impressive however, are the number of significant national publications in Memphis to cover the event.

Tuesday, May 11

5:30 P.M.	Cocktails
	Louis XVI Room
6:30 P.M.	Buffet
	Louis XVI Room
7:30 P.M.	Departure for Reviewing Stand
8:00 P.M.	Arrival of Royal Barge
	Opening Memphis Cotton Carnival
9:00 P.M.	Return to Peabody for Fellowship-Entertainment

Wednesday, May 12

10:00 A.M.	Tour of Memphis
12:00 Noon	Departure for Chattanooga
	Via Chartered American Airlines Convair

GUESTS

Mrs. Josie Stout Thurston
Des Moines Register
Miss Ruth Naomi Knopf
Columbia Broadcasting System
Miss Jo Bradley Reed
Columbus Citizen
Miss Mary Parker
Madamoiselle
Miss Dorothy Wheelock
Harpers Bazaar
Michael Frome
American Automobile Assn.
John Hughes
New York Daily News
James McAdory
Birmingham News
Sylvan Cox
Miami Herald
Herbert H. Beck
Chicago American
E. A. Jones
Highway Traveler
Justin D. Bowersock
Kansas City Star
Fred Burns
Cincinnati Times Star

Claude Talbot
Cleveland News
Robert Ruth
National Geographic Society
Ray W. Gifford
Columbus Dispatch
Harry Smith
Cleveland Plain Dealer
W. Murray Metten
Wilmington News Journal
C. L. Herschel
Washington Post
Myron Glaser
Washington Daily News
Harry Sions
Holiday Magazine
Mr. & Mrs. Frank N. Dunn
Montreal Star
Horace Sutton
The Saturday Review
Mrs. Vera Bradshaw
Household Magazine
Henry Bradshaw
Cappers Farmer

MENU

Decorated Ham to be carved

Decorated Turkey to be carved

Assorted Cold Meats

Assorted Cheese Tray

Italian Spaghetti

Boston Baked Beans

Potatoes au Gratin

Combination Salad
Choice of Dressing

Assorted Celery, Olives, Relishes

Sherbet d'jour, Petit Fours

Coffee - Tea - Milk

Rolls

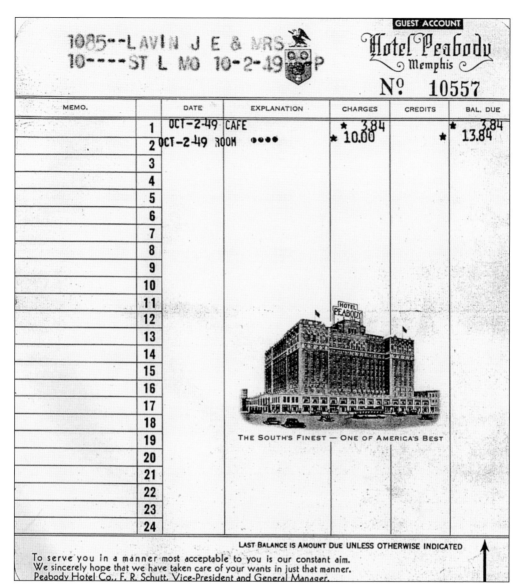

MEMO.		DATE	EXPLANATION	CHARGES	CREDITS	BAL. DUE
	1	OCT-2-49	CAFE	★ 3.84	★	3.84
	2	OCT-2-49	ROOM ••••	★ 10.00	★	13.84
	3					
	4					
	5					
	6					
	7					
	8					
	9					
	10					
	11					
	12					
	13					
	14					
	15					
	16					
	17					
	18					
	19					
	20					
	21					
	22					
	23					
	24					

GUEST ACCOUNT

1085--LAVIN J E & MRS
10----ST L MO 10-2-49 P

Hotel Peabody Memphis

No 10557

THE SOUTH'S FINEST — ONE OF AMERICA'S BEST

LAST BALANCE IS AMOUNT DUE UNLESS OTHERWISE INDICATED

To serve you in a manner most acceptable to you is our constant aim.
We sincerely hope that we have taken care of your wants in just that manner.
Peabody Hotel Co., F. R. Schutt, Vice-President and General Manager.

A 1949 HOTEL BILL. This rare surviving hotel bill from 1949 is one of the many interesting items on display in the hotel's souvenir room on the mezzanine levlel

REGISTRATION DESK. A friendly staff awaited the guest at the registration desk.

THE VENETIAN ROOM. This room has always been the scene of many banquets and festivities.

Three

DAY TO DAY

Hard times were on the horizon for the Memphis landmark. The Memphis Hotel Co., parent company of the Peabody, also owned the Gayoso, the Chisca, and other properties, most of which began losing money. In March 1933, the Memphis Hotel Co. went into receivership and then into bankruptcy. The Peabody, while successful itself, had supplied money for the support of other unprofitable properties under the failing company's umbrella. Money that should have contributed to the Peabody's maintenance and upkeep ended up elsewhere, and the quality of service, as well as the physical condition of the building itself, consequently deteriorated.

Since the Peabody on its own had always been profitable, even during the Depression, it was removed from the list of other corporately owned properties and allowed to stand on its own merits under a reorganization known at the time as the Peabody Hotel Co., Inc, which was owned by four families. The reorganized hotel continued to be managed by Frank Schutt, who also served as vice president. The president of the new operation was Henry Bunn, who had earlier been brought to Memphis from New Orleans to serve as president of the new Lowenstein's Department Store, which had been built on the site of the first Peabody Hotel. Bunn had a long-standing interest in the Peabody Hotel, and had, in fact, spent his wedding night at the first Peabody Hotel, 30 years earlier.

Under the reorganization, the hotel again prospered. The newly decorated Continental Ballroom opened on November 9, 1934, and constant parties, luncheons, conventions, and business meetings again became the order of the day. Crump Stadium opened nearby in 1934 and the Peabody Hotel became the hangout for Ole Miss and other football fans who came to town to see games at the new field. Through it all, the Peabody Hotel had survived and prospered. It made it through partial collapse, the yellow fever epidemic, reconstruction, relocation, the Depression, competition from other hotels, receivership, bankruptcy, and reorganization. But soon, Memphians would turn elsewhere for a social gathering place due to the hotel's increased convention business. The constant presence of large numbers of out-of-towners eventually proved more than the locals could tolerate. Simply put, national conventions ran the locals off, even as the hotel's fame continued to grow throughout America.

PEABODY BALLROOM. Note the architectural attention to detail surrounding the entrance to one of the hotel's grand ballrooms. The most famous quote ever spoken about the Peabody, and still related to this day, is taken from a 1935 book by David Lewis entitled *God Shakes Creation*. In this book, the following is written: "The Mississippi delta begins in the lobby of the Peabody Hotel and ends on Catfish Row in Vicksburg. The Peabody is the Paris Ritz, the Cairo Shepheards, the London Savoy of this section. If you stand near its fountain in the middle of the lobby, where ducks waddle, and turtles drowse, ultimately you will see everybody who is anybody in the delta." The same quote is also attributed to David Cohn, 1935. The statement was well spoken and the point was well taken, regardless of who actually made the observation initially. Today, it is simply stated by Memphians that "the Delta begins in the lobby of the Peabody Hotel." Another, later quote from the *St. Louis Dispatch* of June 1946 by reporter Rufas Terral is: "Mississippians . . . are said to believe that when they die and go to heaven, it will be just like the Peabody lobby." These statements might seem a bit exaggerated today, and yet to those whose lives and fortunes have paralleled those of the Peabody, as well as Memphis itself, such statements do not seem out of the ordinary at all. The Peabody Hotel, Memphis, the Mississippi River, and the people of the city are all interrelated in a finely-woven and colorful tapestry.

PEABODY PLAYING CARDS. The Peabody had its own playing cards.

Another interesting observation is attributed to Clarence Selden, who remarked that during this period (the 1930s), "It was possible to get anything you wanted at the Peabody. You never had to leave." In fact, some people didn't leave. George Landres, a New York merchant who moved to Memphis in 1918 and opened a ladies apparel store on Main Street, lived in the original 1869 Peabody before moving to the present hotel when it opened its doors in 1925. Except for an unsuccessful four-year marriage, he lived in the Peabody until it closed in 1975, a period of slightly more than half a century.

OH, YOU.

COMPLIMENTS OF PEABODY CAFE MEMPHIS, TENN.

GREETING CARD. This greeting card of a little dutch girl was from the Peabody Cafe. The caption on the back reads, "You certainly look good with sparkling eyes of blue. Could you be true? Oh no, not you. C'est me." The Peabody's prosperity and fame continued to grow throughout the World War II years, despite rationing and other deprivations occasioned by the war effort. Soldiers and sailors from nearby bases were permitted to spend the night at no charge in the hotel's lobby, provided they rose early as not to interfere with the hotel's normal operation. The Peabody's financial success continued throughout the decade. In 1948, the Peabody Orchestra was formed to play for the Sunday lunch crowd at the Venetian Room. Local and national bands and orchestras continued to play on the hotel's top floor at the Skyway. For a time, a vocal group consisting of hotel employees daily serenaded guests and their visitors in the lobby during the late afternoon hours from the mezzanine level. After the war, and before the hotel's rebirth and the prosperity of present times, the 1940s may well have been the Peabody's zenith.

THE CONTINENTAL BALLROOM. The Continental Ballroom is as elegant today as it has always been.

THE FAMOUS DUCKS. The ducks appear in front of the marble fountain, which looks the same today as it did in 1925. Who would even think to place ducks in the fountain at one of America's most famous hotels? And why? Actually, what started as an afternoon prank has developed over time into one of the greatest marketing ideas ever created to publicize a business. This has become the stuff of legends and ranks at the top of the marketing chain, along with Chattanooga's famous "See Rock City." Basically, according to tradition, this is what happened: In the past, duck hunters often used live ducks as decoys. Once, as a joke, hotel manager Frank Schutt and friend Chip Barwick put some live decoys in the hotel's fountain after a hunting trip. (Supposedly they'd been drinking a bit.) In any event, this amusing and totally spontaneous action generated a great deal of publicity for the hotel, and it was soon decided that the ducks should remain in the fountain on a permanent basis.

THE FAMOUS DUCKS. At the end of the day, the ducks walk the red carpet back to the elevator which returns them to their "penthouse." In any case, the ducks became an important and permanent feature of the Peabody. Bellman Edward Pembroke, once a circus trainer, offered to escort the ducks to and from the fountain. He was named "Duckmaster" and held that distinguished title from 1940 until his retirement in 1991. And thus a tradition that was inadvertently started, almost as a joke, continues to this day. Every morning at 11 a.m. sharp, the ducks, a drake, and four hens, are brought by elevator from their "penthouse" on the roof and escorted to the fountain in the center of the lobby. Every evening, promptly at 5 p.m., the ducks depart the fountain and ride the elevator back to their rooftop lodgings. Their brief journey is ceremoniously accompanied by marching music and cheers of approval from those gathered to witness this purely Southern tradition which has, over the decades, added to the already considerable reputation of the Peabody Hotel. Due to the initially favorable public response to the ducks, other animals were tried briefly in the fountain, including turtles and even alligators (see above), but it was the ducks that proved most popular. Today they are famous throughout the world. In fact, the ducks traveled to New York where they were presented with the first Lifetime Achievement Special Public Relations Award from the Hospitality, Sales, and Marketing Association International.

TRAVEL ACCOMODATIONS. Edward Pembroke was the original Duckmaster, a title he held until his retirement. He was beloved by all of the staff and guests of the hotel.

The ducks also travel extensively to other parts of America, promoting the Peabody and other Belz properties. While on the road, they enjoy a lifestyle similar to that which they are accustomed to at the Peabody. They're always escorted by an entourage in charge of their accoutrements which include a fabulous carrying cage, their traditional red carpet, and a portable fountain for their swimming comfort. Accommodations invariably include a suite in one of the finest hotels available, whether in New York, Washington, or even Las Vegas. They always travel by jet and are never left unattended in a flimsy cardboard box at the baggage or freight loading platform of some decaying bus station. They are true celebrities and everywhere they go, their appearance creates a sensation. People are always pleasantly surprised and happier for having seen them. At day's end, the ducks are ceremoniously escorted through the Peabody lobby, into the elevator, and to their spacious penthouse atop the Plantation Roof. The new structure was built for them at a cost of $15,000 in 1984. It is 12 feet wide, 18 feet long, and 12.5 feet tall. It was designed by Memphis artist Elinor Hawkins who had worked on the hotel's lobby ceiling and murals. The Royal Duck Palace features an Arabian roof, banners, and a six-foot diameter fountain, as well as murals and a covered bed chamber. The fountain is noteworthy in that it has a centrally placed statue of a large duck with water flowing from its bill.

PLANTATION HOUSE MODEL. This model of the Plantation House in the Royal Duck Palace is a scaled down replica of the much larger version located on the Peabody's celebrated Plantation Roof.

DUCK PENTHOUSE. The fountain located within the ducks' penthouse provides relaxation at the end of a hard day's work swimming in the lobby fountain. The ducks continue to be of great significance to the Peabody, apart from their travels and daily appearances.

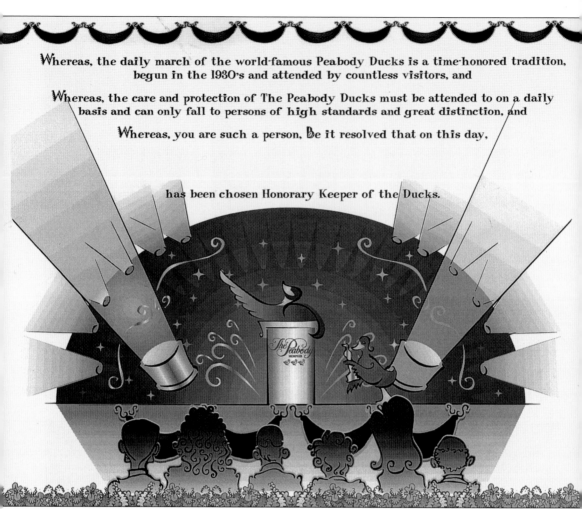

Whereas, the daily march of the world-famous Peabody Ducks is a time-honored tradition, begun in the 1930's and attended by countless visitors, and

Whereas, the care and protection of The Peabody Ducks must be attended to on a daily basis and can only fall to persons of high standards and great distinction, and

Whereas, you are such a person, Be it resolved that on this day,

_____ has been chosen Honorary Keeper of the Ducks.

DUCKMASTER CERTIFICATION. The Duckmaster Certificate is inscribed for the honorary Duckmaster as a souvenir of the occasion. In 1988, the Peabody Honorary Duckmaster Program was initiated. In this event, someone is selected from a visiting convention or meeting, presented with the title of "Honorary Duckmaster," given a t-shirt and cane, and allowed to lead the ducks. This activity always provides an entertaining diversion to the visiting members of any group or meeting, as well as to the hotel's guests. On occasion, a visiting celebrity may serve as guest Duckmaster. But what is truly amazing is that despite the number of times that this twice-daily march of the ducks has occurred over the years, it is always a major event. Guests and visitors invariably begin gathering near the elevators and around the fountain in the morning, awaiting the arrival of the ducks. It is the same at the end of the day as preparations are made for their departure. Even the most experienced traveler is delighted by witnessing their arrival or exit.

CURRENT DUCKMASTER KALYN HOUSDAN. The Duckmaster prepares to return the ducks to the Royal Duck Palace shortly before 5 p.m.

THE PENTHOUSE. The ducks march across the roof to their residence at the end of the day.

Maintenance and improvement at the hotel are constant and seemingly neverending. Beneath the surface elegance of the Peabody lobby and ballrooms there is a vast underworld of wiring, pipes, boilers, and other equipment that are vital to the operation of the hotel. Every guest expects hot water when desired, expects the phones to work every time, and expects everything to be the best available. To insure that this occurs, a full-time staff of engineers and maintenance personnel are always at work. This is as true today as when the hotel was first built. A 1950 newspaper article in the Memphis Press-Scimitar entitled "A Trip Downstairs At the Peabody" described the engineering spaces as follows:

> Underneath Hotel Peabody is a world all by itself-a world of great throbbing engines and generators, turbines, boilers, catwalks and control panels. It's something like the engine room of a battleship. Great polished wheels of the generators, eight feet tall, whirl about ceaselessly pumping the thick pistons which supply power for hotel lights. A puff of white steam escapes with a hiss from one of the three high pressure boilers, great square structures that disappear 25 feet overhead in a maze of pipes, tubes, and steel walkways.
>
> The hotel makes its own electricity, pumps its own water from two wells (450,000 gallons a day), has its own heating and air-conditioning. In case of a city breakdown, the hotel is independent. By the same token, if the hotel equipment ever were to break down, it is hooked up with the city utilities, so the city would supply both water and current. The city is supplying part of the current now, but if the main circuit breaker is thrown, the hotel is ready to take the full load.
>
> Charles G. Moore, 2123 Linden, assistant chief engineer, took a Press-Scimitar reporter on an informal tour. Mr. Moore has been working with engines almost all his life. The pipes and motors under the Peabody are clean and polished. He pointed with pride to one piece of equipment after another. One of three hot water circulating pumps, with the flywheel (at 1740 rpm) whirling around so fast it looked as if it were standing still. These keep hot water the same temperature in all parts of the hotel. Two ice water pumps, three brine pumps (for the cold storage in the kitchens). Three big ammonia compressors. Pumps for two artesian wells. Air-conditioning and vacuuming systems.

As early as 1952, the Peabody installed automatic Otis elevators as part of a $350,000 overall modernization. An automatic elevator—one where you just get on and push a button—is something we all take for granted today. Before its advent however, an elevator attendant, usually uniformed, sat on a very small folding wood seat just inside the elevator door. He or she would manually shut the doors, then pull a floor to ceiling folding brass screen across the door opening. The elevator operator would control the ascent or descent speed with a large brass lever affixed to the side of the elevator wall. As the elevator passed different floors you would see the closed doors of that floor through the brass grating. It was really quite an experience. Sometimes the elevator operator would overshoot the intended floor and have to backup. The elevators jerked and lurched. The addition of automatic passenger elevators, each with walnut paneling and indirect lighting, expedited guest movement in an atmosphere of comfort and elegance. The new passenger elevator, as well as freight elevators, were capable of moving 400 feet per minute on rubber rollers, had center opening doors, and a had capacity of 2,500 pounds each. Another expensive proposition was air conditioning the hotel. This was accomplished over a period of several years and was completed in 1952 at a cost of over $250,000. The first stage of the process was to air condition all of the public areas, including the lobby, mezzanine, restaurants, and the Skyway. Two 250-horsepower compressors were installed in the basement to operate the system. The most difficult part of the project was the replacement of the ceilings in each of the guest rooms to accommodate the air conditioning vents.

NIGHTTIME SCENE. A row of new 1960s Buick convertibles is lined along the side of the Peabody at night.

IN HONOUR OF

HER MAJESTY

Queen Elizabeth II

OF

**ENGLAND AND THE
BRITISH COMMONWEALTH**

CORONATION DAY—JUNE 2, 1953

ʡ

PLANTATION ROOF

HOTEL PEABODY — MEMPHIS, TENN.

THOMAS W. WICKHAM, ESQ.

MENU COVER. Though Queen Elizabeth II was nowhere near Memphis during her coronation, the event provided as good a reason as any for another excellent dinner and celebration in a city famous for dinners, dancing, and celebrations.

Menu

WINES

SCOTCH ... SCOTCH

... SCOTCH and SCOTCH

ʊ

MUSICAL INTERLUDE

"There'll Always Be An England
As Long As Scotland's There"

Poulet a la Southern Belle
Elizabeth
Sauce Prince Charles

Pommes au Gratin Colonial
Pois Verts au Champignons a L'anglais
"Limey" Beans

Salade Verte Buckingham Palace
Sauce Princess Anne

ʊ

Parfait Poor Phillip

ʊ

Tea or Iced!   Rolls a la Piccadi

INSIDE OF MENU.

In 1958, extensive changes in interior decor were made to some of the hotel's 625 rooms. All four of the two-story balconied suites were redecorated. A dozen corner suites and four front suites on the north side from the fifth through the eleventh floors were redone in the traditional style, but with a modern '58' touch. Another 120 rooms had the darker mahogany furniture and traditional beds, dressers, lamps, and artwork replaced with blonde contemporary furniture and modern art paintings. Even more radical styling changes were accomplished in five of the 43 salesmen's sample rooms on the third floor, where the walls were covered in plastic with designs echoed in the curtains. All furniture and lamps were replaced with ultra modern fixtures.

THE VENETIAN DINING ROOM. This room, located on the Mezzanine Level, served lunch

from noon until 2 p.m.

AN ELEGANT CHANDELIER. This chandelier is one of many found throughout the Peabody.

In addition to constant maintenance and frequent remodeling, there is the ongoing financial aspect of operating the hotel. Things took a turn for the worse in the 1950s and many grand downtown hotels suffered despite the booming post-war economy. The Peabody was no exception. In 1952, the first Holiday Inn in the world opened in Memphis on Summer Avenue. In 1953, a second Holiday Inn opened in Memphis, and tourist courts and motor lodges became the new trend nationwide. Downtown traffic and parking were no longer a problem. The new motels had plenty of parking, right in front of patrons' rooms. There was no waiting around for valets, bellboys, or elevators. In fact, for many people, not only in Memphis but nationwide, there was often no need to go downtown at all. By the mid-1950s, a new post-war prosperity had swept the nation. Many Americans were homeowners for the first time due to the G.I. Bill. Many more Americans had cars for the first time and moved away from cities. As they left downtown areas for suburbs, businesses followed. Doctors' offices, department stores, markets, theatres—all businesses that before World War II were almost exclusively found downtown—moved away from the cities. There were other ramifications as well. Railroads began losing passenger travel both to automobiles and airplanes. As air travel increased, hotels began springing up near airports, always located on a city's outskirts. Soon, with revenues dropping, the Peabody was for sale.

Four

HARD TIMES

The Peabody had largely escaped fires, like those which destroyed the nearby Gayoso, but in 1957, the hotel's Continental Ballroom sustained in excess of $100,000 damages in a fire. Another major fire in February 1962 began in an exhaust fan in the engine room and damaged 25 rooms to the extent that they were temporarily unusable. Other minor room fires were started by smokers, while more small fires originated in range vents and engineering spaces. While nobody was killed or even seriously injured in any of these fires, they cast a bad light on the public's perception of the hotel's safety and security.

But an even greater injury to the hotel was about to occur. Frank Schutt, the Peabody's only manager since its 1925 reopening, retired in 1956, a further blow to the hotel. To the Peabody's friends and patrons, he and the hotel were one and the same. He had been responsible for the famous ducks in the fountain, the summer dances on the roof, the construction of the Skyway, and many other things which were so much a part of the Peabody. He was basically irreplaceable.

So competition from other hotels, newer motels, the loss of the hotel's longtime manager, mismanagement from the hotel's new ownership, and fire all combined to take their toll on the Peabody's fortunes during the 1950s. Other internal changes caused further loss of local patronage. The hotel management closed the basement coffee shop, a Memphis tradition, in 1955, and rented the entire basement to television station WREC, for use as a studio. The Cadet Room, the Peabody's most popular lunchroom, was shut down and the space rented to the Petroleum Club. Then, in 1957, the hotel's elegant and famous dining facility, the Venetian Room, was permanently closed. This Memphis landmark was famous all over the South and its closing likely angered and offended local patrons. It probably seemed to many Memphians that the hotel's management was almost trying to run people off.

Other significant social changes had taken place that affected the Peabody's financial status. Fast food restaurants and drive-ins had become increasingly visible on the national landscape, and in Memphis, too. Students from Ole Miss, Southwestern, and Memphis State now sought social life and entertainment in places other than the Peabody. Music had also changed drastically, and Memphis, with its Sun Records, was in the forefront of the American music revolution. The orchestras and bands of the 1920s, 1930s, and 1940s, those which had once filled the Peabody's Skyway and Plantation Roof, were now obsolete, and the large formal parties, the type so frequently held at the Peabody in the past, had become much less common.

The growing trend towards modernism was reflected in every aspect of American life. From fashion, to space-age appliances and furniture, to streamlined futuristic cars which resembled rockets and spaceships, everything was moving quickly away from classicism. Antique furniture, giant houses, and large hotels like the Peabody were no longer considered to be grand and elegant, but rather old and obsolete. In 1958, the Downtowner Corporation opened a modern 120-room hotel on Union, right across the street from the Peabody, providing a modern downtown hotel with free parking. Other newer and more convenient motels soon opened in Memphis, including the Admiral Benbow on Union, a Howard Johnson's near the airport, and another Holiday Inn.

The next change the hotel faced was integration. It opened its doors to black patrons in 1961, but the move was not without consequences. Memphis was then a highly segregated city, and socialites of the era were not prepared to accept such radical changes literally (they felt) overnight. The loss in revenue was immediate. In the 1961–1962 year the Peabody lost $245,700 in profits. The next year saw a further drop of $78,000. Basically the hotel was abandoned by the Memphis upper crust as a result of its inclusive policy toward African Americans. But the hotel and the black population of Memphis had always had a close bond. Of the hotel's approximately 900 permanent employees in 1951, 650 were African-American and many had positions of great responsibility. While it would be incorrect to say that racial prejudice did not exist in the South, or even in the Peabody, the hotel did promote blacks. Hosea Wright, the Peabody's 44-year-old executive chef, spent 28 years at the hotel prior to its bankruptcy. He started as a dishwasher, then became coffee maker, short order cook, roast cook, first cook, chef's steward, and finally executive chef. In any case, the Memphis bon ton felt forced to look elsewhere for a place to hold their meetings and parties. Newer hotels and motels opened, and for a time sufficed, but none of these newer facilities possessed the grace, charm, or traditions of the Peabody. Ultimately, everybody lost.

But it wasn't just integration that brought the Peabody to its knees—it was the overall change occurring in the South. The agricultural economy had been largely replaced by a fast-paced business world. Edward Pembroke, the Peabody's original Duckmaster and superintendent of hotel services, summed it up this way: "Farming's gone, the salesmen travel by plane, come in here and do a million dollar's worth of business and go back the same day. Everybody's giving free parking and this (the Peabody) is just not built for that. It's common sense."

In addition to substantial lost revenue, the hotel was faced with massive debts, including a first mortgage in excess of $2,000,000 owed to the Equitable Life Assurance Society of America, another $337,500 to the Memphis National Bank of Commerce, and $876,199 due to former stockholders as a third mortgage. Add to these figures interest debts of $175,000 and past due taxes of $95,000 and it is easy to see why the Peabody was in trouble.

By 1965 it was over, at least for the moment. Attempts to refinance and reorganize the hotel's debts failed and Judge Bailey Brown approved plans for a foreclosure sale. Delta Auction Company was chosen to conduct the sale and an auction date was set for Tuesday December 14, at noon at the Shelby County Courthouse. Delta at that time had offices in Ft. Worth, Houston, Dallas, Baton Rouge, and New Orleans as well as executive offices in Memphis. The Peabody was subsequently bought by the Alsonett hotel chain in July 1953 for $7,495,000. This group also owned Memphis's famous King Cotton and more than 30 other hotel properties throughout the nation. In an effort to compete with the parking facilities of the new motels, Alsonett bought a parking garage in 1954 for $480,000. And yet, the Peabody did not fare well under Alsonett's management. Again, the revenue generated by the Peabody helped support other properties to its own detriment. Personal service to customers and the former espirit d' corps, which had always characterized the employees and staff, diminished as well. And there were other problems, too.

HARD TIMES. The Town Park Motor Hotel, the "Pride of Memphis" featured 150 air conditioned rooms, a swimming pool, 24-hour room service, and television—in short, every amenity of the best hotels of the time, without the problems of downtown traffic and parking.

ALSONETT
HOTELS

TUA DOMUS   TUUM CASTELLUM

Alsonett Hotels

MATCHBOOK COVER FROM THE PEABODY'S ALSONETT PERIOD.

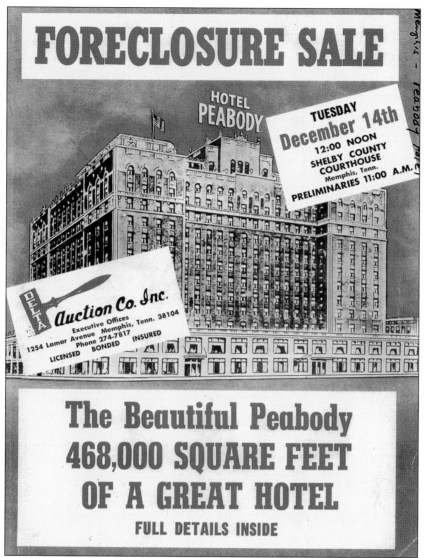

FORECLOSURE SALE

HOTEL
PEABODY

TUESDAY
December 14th
12:00 NOON
SHELBY COUNTY
COURTHOUSE
Memphis, Tenn.
PRELIMINARIES 11:00 A.M.

DELTA **Auction Co. Inc.**
Executive Offices
1254 Lamar Avenue Memphis, Tenn. 38104
Phone 274-7817
LICENSED BONDED INSURED

The Beautiful Peabody
468,000 SQUARE FEET
OF A GREAT HOTEL
FULL DETAILS INSIDE

FORECLOSURE SALE BROCHURE. This foreclosure sale brochure was sent to prospective buyers. As is common in cases where an expensive and nationally known property is to be auctioned, an informative and detailed brochure was compiled about the hotel and mailed to interested parties. The auction brochure is a true collectible piece of Memphis memorabilia. It was very detailed and sought not only to present the hotel in its most favorable light, but to portray the City of Memphis as "the second fastest-growing city in the entire South."

Despite the sad state of affairs the Peabody was in at the time, the general consensus in Memphis was that someone would buy the hotel and that it would be open again soon under new management. There may have been some doubt that the hotel would again regain its former status, but there was little doubt that the Peabody would be open forever. It was an integral part of Memphis life.

THE FAMOUS LOBBY FOUNTAIN. The marble fountain, centerpiece of the lobby, is as beautiful and elegant today as when it was first seen by the public in 1925.

THE GOVERNOR'S SUITE. Shown here is an interior view of the Governor's Suite as it appeared in the mid-1970s.

Despite occasional returns to past glory, matters had not turned out well for the elegant Peabody after all, despite the large financial expenditure by Sheraton. The hotel was purchased by James Lane, an Alabama hotelier in January 1974, but was placed in bankruptcy on March 31 of the same year and closed at the end of the following business day, April 1. With just 53 registered guests out of a total of 617 available rooms, the hotel simply could not make ends meet. An April 1975 article in the *Memphis Press Scimitar* lamented the hotel's sad circumstances and suggested that the city's leadership "turn its attention to keeping the Peabody open as a modern and profitable downtown enterprise."

A Section of the Presidential Suite, mid-1970s. The famous presidential suite was elegant for its time.

Five

SAVED BY THE BELZES:
THE TRADITION CONTINUES

It was speculated in early 1975 that the Sheraton hotel chain might actually tear down the Peabody altogether, and Sheraton officials would not comment. What was certain was that during that very period, Sheraton was dismantling the famous 804-room Sheraton-Gibson Hotel in Cincinnati. The words of a Memphis hotel and motel appraiser did not inspire confidence when he said that "the Peabody is only worth the land it's sitting on." The undisclosed principal turned out to be Belz Investment Co., Tennessee's largest real estate development company, in partnership with Edwin Hanover, Jack Belz's father-in-law. While Belz was prepared to offer a substantial amount of its own money, the overall project was extensive and would require more money than the hotel had ever received. Restoration costs were expected to reach nearly $12,000,000. A substantial loan or loans would be required to finance the project. There were both public and private speculation that the hotel might not be a financially viable entity no matter how much money was spent or what steps were taken. If a company with the size and market power, and financial strength of Sheraton couldn't make the hotel a financial success, what chance did anyone else have? Simply put, this perception would have to be overcome if adequate financing was to be obtained from any source.

Plans for the renovation included reducing the number of hotel rooms from 617 to 400, thus increasing room size and creating some new suites. The projected cost of $25,000 to $28,000 per room, as expensive as it was, would still be far less than the cost per room of building a new hotel from the ground up. Immediately, a group of various interests spearheaded by the Belz family and Sen. Jim Sasser began seeking to add the Peabody to the National Register of Historic Places. An application was filed by Jim Williamson of Keith Kays and Associates, which had obtained similar status for other Memphis properties, notably the Orpheum Theatre and the D.T. Porter Building, the city's first tall building. In September 1977, the Peabody was added to that long and noble list. Being on the National Register is not a guarantee that a building will not be torn down, as some people incorrectly believe. It simply means that no federal funds may be used in a building's demolition without a review at a national level. On the other hand, being on the list officially confers a certain prestige and status which, while it may have existed before, becomes nationally recognized upon inclusion in the list. Being added to this list also makes the honored building, in theory at least, eligible for matching funds from the National Park Service, and offers certain tax advantages. It also, in theory, makes a property's restoration more appealing to a bank or other lending institution.

As far as funding for the Peabody project, the Belz family had been waiting for two years at the time the Peabody made the National Register. They had already invested nearly a million dollars in the project including the purchase of the hotel and a parking facility. Expenses of insurance, security, taxes, and utilities were running in excess of $20,000 per month. Something needed to happen soon if the hotel was to be saved at all.

A campaign of public awareness had been launched as soon as the hotel was purchased. The more people who wanted the hotel saved, the better. The press were very supportive as well, with nearly weekly articles from the *Press-Scimitar* and the *Commercial Appeal* keeping the Memphis landmark constantly in the public eye. The hotel hosted a $10 a person "Return to the Peabody—a Memphis Memory" in October 1977, an event sponsored by the Memphis Heritage Association and Ballet South. More than 700 people attended the successful benefit for Ballet South, and for an evening it was like old times at the hotel lobby. Even ducks had been specially trained by the original Duckmaster, Edward Pembroke, and returned to the fountain for the evening. By the end of July 1978, however, nearly three years after the hotel had been purchased by the Belz family, the necessary financing had still not been approved. A controlled sale with an admission price of $2 was announced, offering much of the hotel's interior furnishings for sale to the public. The sale, handled by ABC Liquidators, was set to start on July 26, 1978. It would last two months and hopefully raise $300,000. Items for sale included 400 televisions, hotel china and crystal, beds, rollaway beds, chairs, sofas, restaurant tables, coffee tables, desks, end chairs, and assorted linens, including monogrammed blankets, new and used sheets, towels, and bedspreads. A crowd of approximately 1,800 arrived on opening day, including a large number of curiosity seekers. By the end of August, most of what merchandise still remained had been moved to the lobby. The sale ran daily, including weekends.

Finally, in November 1978, after nearly three and a half years of constant effort by the Belz Investment Co., there was a light at the end of the tunnel A loan commitment was signed between Belz and two Memphis banks for $7,500,000 of the $10,000,000 needed to completely redo the hotel's interior. The deal was with First Tennessee Bank and the National Bank of Commerce, which agreed to loan the money at 8.9 percent for 22 years, providing certain other conditions were met. Two of these conditions were that the Federal Economic Development Agency would have to guarantee 90 percent of the loan, and that a third bank, lending institution, or other source, would have to supply the other $2,500,000 needed to complete the project. There were still other hoops to jump through before construction could actually start—approval of a tax reduction, approval by the city building and fire inspectors, approval of the state's historical register board, and bids from contractors capable of performing the work. This was in addition to the nearly $3,000,000 of Belz's own money already committed to the project.

So far, Belz Investment Co. had absorbed all of the risks involved with the undertaking of the very difficult Peabody project. Now the company needed the help of the city to bring the restoration to completion. Belz asked that Memphis close a section of Gayoso Avenue and donate it to the hotel for parking space. This was, for Belz, the deal breaker. The hotel could not operate as a modern facility without adequate on-site parking. The Center City Commission, the Land Use Control Board, and the city's administration all agreed, and the Memphis City Council voted to cede the land to the hotel. But even this was not without problems for the Belz Co. If substantial renovation work was not started by October 1979, or if the hotel ceased operation for 120 consecutive days, the land would revert to the city. Additionally, there was substantial opposition from nearby businesses who complained that closing the street would create great inconveniences. Last but not least, certain individuals and groups felt that giving public land to a private business was unfair to other individuals and businesses.

When the restored Peabody reopened in 1981, the public was introduced to the completed project, unaware for the most part of the detailed planning and extensive work that had taken place behind the scenes. The restoration of the hotel was, however, a massive undertaking which involved significant structural and design changes as well as input from a very large group of experts in a variety of fields, including electricians, plumbers, engineers, interior decorators and designers, historians, researchers, and restaurant consultants, among others. All in all, there were a total of 21 consultants. Keeping all of their efforts coordinated and focused was a major task in itself. Before any of the restoration could begin however, the architectural plans had to be formulated.

Jack Belz met with Memphis architect Jack McFarland, who had worked with the Belzes on other projects, and after an interview, selected him to oversee the restoration of the hotel. Jack McFarland was probably the most qualified architect in the South for this project, mainly because of his prior experience with hotel restoration and reconfiguration. More significantly for the Peabody project in particular was his experience with other Memphis hotels from the same period. Specifically, he'd worked on the project which had taken the former Claridge Hotel, basically gutted it, and completely reconfigured it as an apartment building. The Hotel Chisca, another large downtown Memphis hotel, had also been modernized as an earlier project he had been involved with.

For the duration of the Peabody's restoration, the project was a work in progress, not just in the sense that progress was being made, but in that plans changed frequently in many cases as the overall project advanced. As an example, Architect Jack McFarland recalls that the small but elegant Board Room for the hotel's board of directors, which is located on the Mezzanine level, was reworked on three separate occasions before it was completed. And then there were the guest rooms. The plan was to reduce the original number of rooms from more than 600 to no more than 400, basically a reduction of almost one-third, a significant number by any standard. The reason for the reduction in number was to increase the size of individual rooms. During the 50 years since the 1925 Peabody had opened, the public had grown to expect larger, more comfortable rooms. Reworking the number and size of the rooms within the finite space of the hotel presented some interesting architectural and engineering problems. The hotel had been constructed, as was the custom in the 1920s, of large steel beams with structural clay tile vertical walls. The clay tile walls separating guest rooms, as a rule, were three inches thick. Then, an inch of plaster was applied on each side of the tile, producing a standard five-inch-thick vertical wall. Additionally, the steel beams, both vertical and horizontal, were encased in structural clay tile. To complicate matters, the room arrangement was not always consistent from floor to floor. Essentially, walls were removed and smaller rooms were combined, creating a single, larger room, without altering the steel framework. This process produced its own set of problems, especially where the elaborate plaster cornices were involved. In the restoration or modernization of many older commercial buildings, existing ceiling height is often lowered by suspending a different type of ceiling from the original. In the case of the Peabody, the original ceiling height was maintained, and the original ceilings were all either repaired or replaced. But again, the plaster work was more elaborate and extensive in some rooms than in others, and some had been damaged by water over the years.

MEMPHIS ARCHITECT JACK MCFARLAND. McFarland (right) was the lead architect in the restoration of the Peabody. He is seen here as president of the Tennessee Society of Architects at a meeting in Nashville in 1971.

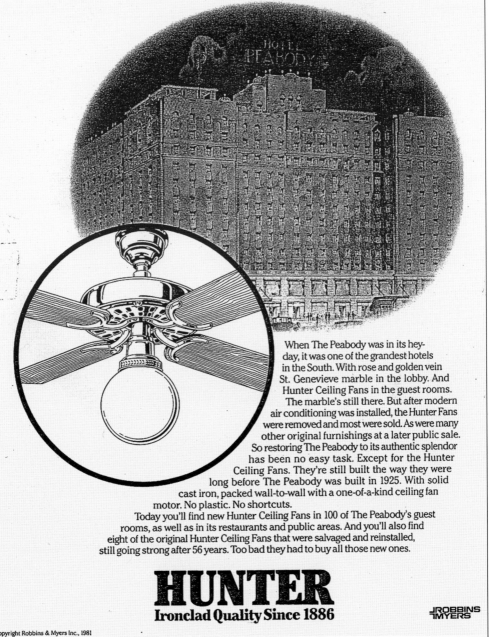

Hotels just aren't built the way they used to be.

Fortunately for The Peabody, Hunter Ceiling Fans still are.

When The Peabody was in its heyday, it was one of the grandest hotels in the South. With rose and golden vein St. Genevieve marble in the lobby. And Hunter Ceiling Fans in the guest rooms. The marble's still there. But after modern air conditioning was installed, the Hunter Fans were removed and most were sold. As were many other original furnishings at a later public sale. So restoring The Peabody to its authentic splendor has been no easy task. Except for the Hunter Ceiling Fans. They're still built the way they were long before The Peabody was built in 1925. With solid cast iron, packed wall-to-wall with a one-of-a-kind ceiling fan motor. No plastic. No shortcuts.

Today you'll find new Hunter Ceiling Fans in 100 of The Peabody's guest rooms, as well as in its restaurants and public areas. And you'll also find eight of the original Hunter Ceiling Fans that were salvaged and reinstalled, still going strong after 56 years. Too bad they had to buy all those new ones.

HUNTER
Ironclad Quality Since 1886

ROBBINS MYERS

HUNTER FANS. These fans are built in Memphis, and are in their own way as much a tradition in the South as the Peabody.

PEABODY BAR. A new full service bar was placed at one end of the lobby and serves as a

gathering place for locals and visitors alike.

INTRICATE DETAILS. The detailed wood and plaster work of the lobby and mezzanine were returned to their original grandeur. With restoration nearing completion, a new staff was hired and trained to provide the level of personal service that the Peabody had been noted for. With everything in place, the famous Peabody Ducks were returned to the fountain under the watchful care of Edward Pembroke, who had been responsible for them since 1940. At last, after six years, with the restoration complete, the Peabody opened again on September 1, 1981. The reopening was 56 years to the day that the 1925 building had opened at the same Union and Third location. As might be imagined, a Peabody-style celebration began in the morning with the arrival of Sen. Jim Sasser, and Mayors Wyeth Chandler and Bill Morris in horse-drawn carriages accompanied by a marching band. There were speeches from local dignitaries, members of the Belz family, and others, followed by an invitation-only luncheon for 300 people at the Continental Ballroom. The festivities continued throughout the day with a midnight champagne buffet for 450, and a grand opening dinner dance from 8 to 12 at the Skyway.

GUEST ROOMS. The rooms at the Peabody are always comfortable and inviting.

PLANS FOR PEABODY PLACE. As early as 1986, plans were fully in the works for Peabody Place, as this overview of the city shows, with the darkened area representing the proposed location for the development. This massive retail center opened in 2001 and features in excess of 300,000 square feet of specialty and entertainment shops, several theme restaurants, a 22-screen

movie complex, and an IMAX Theatre.In addition, there are many other entertainment and retail venues that provide an elegant and superb place for citizens and visitors to socialize and celebrate.

THE SKYWAY. The Skyway has been completely restored to its original appearance and is still the venue of choice for great entertainment, a private party, or celebration.

MAIN STREET, 1906. Today, trolleys again travel north and south on Main Street, just as they did in 1906 when this postcard was mailed.

The Lobby Under Restoration.

THE RESTORED LOBBY. This photo was taken before the installation of the new furniture. The elegant design is clearly apparent in this photograph taken from the Mezzanine level.

FOOD SERVICE. The food services at the Peabody have always been legendary.

BEHIND THE SCENES. Preparations for one of the many conventions and banquets at the Peabody.

PEABODY FEATURES

Belz Enterprises began in the 1940s when company founder Philip Belz developed six acres in north Memphis into a warehouse complex. From these humble beginnings more than half a century ago, Belz Enterprises has developed into one of the largest real estate developers in America. Today, Memphis based Belz Enterprises owns and manages more than 25 million square feet of shopping centers, hotels, office buildings, and warehouse space. Today, Jack Belz, son of the late founder, continues to operate the company founded by his father, along with third-generation family members (sons Martin Belz, Ronald Belz, and son-in-law Andy Groveman). They, along with other executives, share responsibility for the various divisions of this large company.

PEABODY PLACE MUSEUM AND GALLERY. This unique and beautiful museum and gallery originally opened on October 15, 1998 as a 7,500-square-foot facility housing a wide variety of rare and exquisite Chinese artifacts and selected items from the extensive personal collection of Jack and Marilyn Belz. It has since been expanded to 12,000 square feet and now additionally includes Italian mosaics, Judaica, exotic minerals and specimens, Russian lacquered boxes, and priceless works of art from other categories. Among the many rare and one-of-a-kind artifacts on display are exquisite Chinese lacquered chairs, delicately carved jade, agate, and ivory pieces, many of extreme antiquity. This museum is something which must be seen. One cannot help but marvel at the items on display. The intricacy and detail of some of the ivory carvings is almost beyond description. The museum is located in the Pembroke Building at 119 South Main and is open daily except Monday.

CLOISONNE TEMPLE LION. This Cloisonne Temple Lion or "Foo Dog" is nearly six feet tall and one of a pair on display that once stood watch over the Forbidden City.

125

LANSKY AT THE PEABODY. The Lansky name in Memphis has been synonymous with cutting edge fashions in the Bluff City for more than 50 years. In fact, it was Lansky's on Beale Street where Elvis shopped for many of his most distinctive clothes. This famous shop, now located in the Peabody lobby, features the very latest in men's fashions from some of the worlds foremost brands and designers. Names like Jhane Barnes, Tommy Bahama (also women's), Robert Talbott, Kenneth Cole, Nicole Miller, Coogi and Tundra, Mezlan, Donald Pliner, and many more are featured. You are always welcome to shop or browse through the many wonderful selections. And while you're there, enjoy the autographed guitars of the many famous musicians who shop and visit Lansky at the Peabody (901-529-9070).

LANSKY—CLOTHES THAT ROCK. This store was created to share the Memphis Music experience with guests and visitors who have come to the city to enjoy and participate in the musical heritage of the "Birthplace of the Blues." This unique store offers the very latest and best selection of Memphis and Peabody souvenirs as well as a wide selection of gifts for that special someone back home. The walls of the store are filled with great music memorabilia for sale, including autographed photos of a variety of famous artists from B.B. King to Mick Jagger. In addition to souvenirs, there are also plenty of clothes available. If you are looking for the coolest t-shirt, or a hip ball cap, you will find it here along with some really neat retro-style shirts with music notes or guitars woven into the fabric. The Lansky Brothers "Clothier to the King" Boutique is also featured inside this store and offers some of the very same shirts Elvis bought from the original Lansky store on Beale Street. If the King were living today there is no doubt he would be wearing many of the new styles featured in this store. (901-405-7625 or www.lanskybros.com).

THE LUCKY DUCK. The perfect gift shop with anything and everything having to do with ducks! This exciting shop is located in the hotel lobby right next door to the elevator that each day transports the famous Peabody Ducks to and from the magnificent marble fountain where they pleasantly pass their days swimming around the centerpiece. In answer to the constant demand for Peabody souvenirs, The Lucky Duck is stocked with a wide variety of top brand name merchandise emblazoned with the distinctive Peabody Hotel logo. From beautiful Turkish robes and one-of-a-kind wooden ducks, to coffee mugs, sleep shirts, "Legend of the Duck'" t-shirts, and duck items of all types, there is something for everyone. A great selection of merchandise is also available for children, including plush stuffed ducks, infant wear, toys, and children's books that tell the story of the famous Peabody Ducks. The finest in gifts and souvenirs is also available including Swarovski Crystal, Lladro Figurines, Christopher Radko Ornaments, and many more. (901-432-0943 or www.peabodyducks.com).

MR. B's ESSENTIALS. This is the place to go to start or end your day with the right magazine, the *New York Times*, or the *Wall Street Journal*. There are also a wide variety of personal toiletries including razors, shampoo, aspirin, and other items always on hand. For the smoker, a fine selection of premium cigars is available. In addition to being the Birthplace of Soul, and Rock N' Roll, the Home of the Blues, and much more musically, Memphis is also the barbecue capital of the world. To that end Mr. B's Essentials stocks the *Great Memphis Bar-B-Que Cookbook* as well as sauce and seasonings from the world famous Rendezvous. Fresh "Made in Memphis" candies, yellow chocolate ducks, Jack Daniel's Tipsy Cakes, and other delectable treats will give you the perfect taste of Memphis.

Appropriate gifts are available in large quantities for convention visitors. Convention managers and tour planners should call for help in arranging the perfect Peabody gift. (901-844-1913).

In addition to the Lansky shops, there are other retail merchants whose shops are located within the Peabody Hotel itself, including the Northwest Airlines office.